Becoming a GovCon Expert

How to Accelerate Your Success in Government Contracting

Michael LeJeune and Joshua P. Frank

Contributing Authors

Russ Barnes, PhD
Systro Solutions

Jenny Clark
Solvability

Joshua P. Frank
RSM Federal

Emily Harman
Emily Harman Coaching and Consulting

Michael LeJeune
RSM Federal

Eric "Doc" Wright, PhD
Vets2PM

Requests to the Publisher for permission should be addressed to RSM Federal, 13 Amber Wave Ct. O'Fallon, MO 63366 or contact@rsmfederal.com. Liability / Disclaimer: Although the author has used his best efforts in preparing this book, he makes no representations or warranties with respect to the accuracy or completeness of the contents of this book.

No warranty may be created or extended by sales representatives, strategic partners, affiliates, or written sales collateral. The lessons, recommendations, and strategies contained in this book may not be applicable to your specific business requirements. You should consult with a professional consultant where appropriate. The author shall not be liable for any loss of revenue or profit or incidental damages. For more information about RSM Federal, visit www.rsmfederal.com. For more information about the authors, visit www.authorjoshfrank.com and www.michaellejeune.com

ISBN 978-1-7336009-6-5 (pbk)
ISBN 978-1-7336009-7-2 (ebk)

Printed in the United States of America
1 2 3 4 5 6 7 8 9 10

Other Books by RSM Federal Publishing

#1 Amazon Bestseller - An Insider's Guide to Winning Government Contracts
https://bit.ly/GovConInsidersGuide

#1 Amazon Bestseller - Game Changers for Government Contractors
https://bit.ly/GovConGameChangers

The Government Sales Manual
https://bit.ly/GovConSalesManual

v

Contents

Foreword

By Christopher Craig

Board Director at Unanet and Capture2Proposal

The experts who have authored this book have spent their careers working with government contractors to support their objectives. They have written a compelling text for anyone who is currently a government contractor or looking to move into the industry. Key topics of the book include leadership, capture, business development, common challenges, compliance, and accounting.

I have worked with government contractors for twenty-five years, and I continue to be impressed by the people I meet and the services and solutions they deliver to our nation. I trust you will enjoy reading this book, and learning more about all the facets of government contracting, along with its abundance of acronyms, from the book's knowledgeable contributors!

Government contractors play a critical role in everything from securing our nation's defense, supporting our troops overseas and at home, optimizing energy usage and healthcare, exploring space and beyond, fostering education for our nation's youth, researching new technologies, and countless other areas. These government contracting companies are absolutely essential to achieve the government's mission through the delivery of literally everything from sophisticated cyber security services and medical studies, to the more mundane ammunition procurement and janitorial services. While contractors often receive a negative reputation from the media, e.g. Edward Snowden, the movie "War Dogs", etc., the truth is that the vast majority of contractors work tirelessly hand in glove with government employees to ensure successful outcomes. They are truly patriots enabling the United States to thrive!

There are tremendous career paths for those looking to enter federal contracting. The various forecasts for federal government procurement for 2020 was just north of $600,000,000,000. This represented an astonishing approximate one third of the United States' Gross Domestic Product (GDP); quite a sizable customer! While the Department of Defense (DoD) is responsible for about one-half of the obligated dollars, the other major civilian customers are the Departments of Energy, Veterans Affairs, Health & Human Services, Homeland Security, National Aeronautics and Space Administration, and General Services Administration.

Many citizens recognize the names of the largest contractors like Lockheed Martin, Boeing, General Dynamics, Northrop Grumman, and Raytheon, while many are unaware of the amount of small and mid-size businesses that the government depends upon. The top ten federal contractors receive roughly 30% of the government's prime contracts. Small businesses, according to the government's definition, make up 25% of the government's prime contracts, and the government sets aside specific contracts for small business in order to foster their growth and enable them to compete with the large "primes". Types of small business "set asides" include 8(a) (Disadvantaged), HUBZone, Women-Owned, and Service-Disabled Veteran Owned.

The total number of contractors employed by the federal government is estimated to fluctuate between 4,000,000 and 5,000,000. All of this means there is an incredible opportunity for those looking to work with the government!

The vast majority of government contracting takes place in Washington, D.C., and the surrounding suburbs of Maryland and Virginia. That said, there are plenty of other areas throughout the country that are hot spots for federal contracting. These include San Diego, Huntsville, Colorado Springs, Atlanta, Austin, Houston, Tampa, Charleston, Dayton and many others. Certainly, contractors are also deployed in almost every country as well. A significant amount of government contractors are able to work remotely although there are many others that are required to work onsite due to security regulations.

As is similar to the government itself, government contractors deal with a variety of acronyms. Throughout the book, you will see terms like FAR (Federal Acquisition Regulation), DCAA (Defense Contract Audit Agency), CMMC (Cybersecurity Maturity Model Certification), and countless others. You need not be intimidated by these terms as they are easily referenced on the Internet.

Selling to the government is extremely different from a typical business sales process. Key characteristics of success include patience and diligence. The authors in this book will guide you through navigating the plethora of opportunities solicited by the government, evaluating what is realistic for your business, developing competitive pricing, and writing a winning proposal.

Once you begin winning government contracts, you will need to execute on and perform for the contract. This also means you will need to track and account for the work performed. The concept of indirect costs can (and should) be applied to any commercial business, and the government requires tracking these costs (e.g. fringe, overhead, G&A) by law. Basically, this means allocating a portion of your fringe benefits, your rent, and your finance team, as examples, into your overall profitability.

I am writing this Foreword because I believe in the benefits that government contractors deliver to our country, I believe in the authors' expertise, and I remain active in the government contracting community as a Board Director at Unanet and with Capture2Proposal.

Enjoy the read!

Christopher Craig

Introduction

First off, on behalf of all of my co-authors, I want to thank you for buying a copy of this book. While it's just a small investment, it means the world to our team that you invested your hard earned money with us. With that in mind, our objective of this book is to create a massive return on investment for you.

I'd like to set some expectations for you. This book is just the first step on your journey to becoming a GovCon expert. It's impossible for our team to cover everything there is to know about GovCon in one book. In fact, many of my co-authors have written their own books and the links for these can be found throughout the book. I highly suggest you check them out along with their other resources. Speaking of other resources, in addition to books, most of our co-authors also have a podcast. Links to those podcasts will also be at the end of their bio's or mentioned elsewhere in this book.

As you can already see, we often make mention of other resources. Most of these resources are FREE or similar to the cost of this book. So take advantage of these resources and take advantage of the knowledge provided.

Who Are the GovCon Experts?

Good question. Why should you trust us? You likely picked up this book because you know one of us, but you may not know all of us. Let me take a quick minute to tell you about all of my co-authors.

Russ Barnes (Intention) of Systro Solutions, is the author of Small Business for Service Members and Executive Coach for The Purposefully Profitable™ Program, a strategy development service that puts small business owners in control of their ability to achieve desired outcomes with their companies. https://www.systro.org/purposefully-profitable-program/

Jenny Clark (Connection) of Solvability, is the host of #FreedomFriday, that has created an online community for veterans, entrepreneurs and business leaders in federal contracting and bridges veterans in the defense community to infinite pathways to relationships and resources. https://solvability.com/

Joshua Frank (Acceleration) of RSM Federal, referred to as "The Professor of Government Sales," is an award-winning business coach, professional speaker, multi-best-selling author including the _Insider's Guide to Winning Government Contracts_, available on Amazon, that arms you with step-by-step strategies, concepts, and recommendations for winning government contracts. https://rsmfederal.com

Emily Harman (Authenticity) is the host of the Onward Podcast and Founder of the Onward Movement, whose goal is to inspire 10,000 others to bravely embrace authenticity and release the fear of judgment so you can pursue your dreams with confidence. https://emilyharman.com/

Michael LeJeune (Game Changer) of RSM Federal, is host of the Game Changers Podcast, a government podcast designed to help government contractors find and win more contracts. Each Game Changers episode brings new techniques and strategies from leading national experts with extensive backgrounds in small business federal acquisition. https://rsmfederal.com

Eric "Doc" Wright, PhD (Fluency) of Vets2PM, teaches veteran and small business owners how to become fluent in the language of business so they realize more revenue, profitability, productivity, competitive advantage, and longevity. https://vets2pm.com/

What to Expect

You should expect to be blown away. One of the things I love about this book is that you are going to get _techniques and strategies from different, but similar points of view_. A good example is that we have two chapters about leadership from two different authors. Each of these chapters provide enormous value and a unique view of the key ingredients that make powerful leaders.

Expect to take a lot of notes. In fact, I recommend that you grab a notepad and a pen before you dig into chapter 1. You are going to need it. Use these notes as your action item list.

You are going to have a lot of 'aha' moments. You may even kick yourself a few times as you discover mistakes you've already made. That's OK. Learn and know better next time.

You may find yourself a little overwhelmed with all of the tips and advice. That's OK. Keep building your action item list and then simply prioritize the most important ones. If you apply just ONE strategy per week, that's 52 strategies in a year. Maybe you can't handle one per week? If not, complete one action item per month. That still translates into 12 strategies a year. Long-term success is not about doing everything right now. It's about continually making progress toward your goals, even if it's one little step each month. Keep moving forward.

If you find yourself overwhelmed, PLEASE reach out to one of us. I cannot tell you how much I respect each and every co-author in this book. My words can't do justice. But what I can tell you is that my coauthors are some of the *kindest, down-to-earth, and caring people you will ever meet*. They will return your email or phone call. So don't be afraid to reach out to any of us. In fact, one of your first action items should be to connect on LinkedIn with each and every one of the authors.

Thanks Jenny!

Before we get started, I want to take a minute to thank Jenny Clark for pulling this team of experts together. Jenny is known as the Oprah of GovCon because she knows EVERYONE in this community. She also has one of the biggest hearts you will ever find. Her compassion for people and her love of the GovCon community make her an invaluable asset to all of us.

And with that, it's time to begin your journey toward Becoming a GovCon Expert! Have fun and enjoy!

Michael LeJeune
Editor-in-Chief

YOUR FOUNDATION

Chapter 1.
Preparing Yourself to Succeed in Doing Business with the Government

By Russ Barnes

Founder, Systro Solutions

To know thyself is the beginning of wisdom. - Socrates

Personal development precedes business development. Doing business with the government is no exception. This chapter is tailored to government contracting, but the concepts apply to business in general because *in order to do business with the government, you have to be able to do business.*

Everything a business needs to run, the government needs as well. The government spends trillions of dollars every year on products and services. Some people think government contracting is a gravy train. Nothing could be further from the truth. Doing business with the government is similar to doing business with a non-government client. Whether your business model is business to consumer or business to business, your clients have a problem which they pay you to solve. That's as simple as it gets, but that doesn't mean it's easy. It's not. Government contracting requires you to have a keen understanding of funding, contracts, hiring, timelines and business development at a minimum.

If you decide to make government contracting your first business venture, then you need to know how the government views your value, which means first you have to be clear on how you assess your own value. Successfully doing business with the government is based on your ability to demonstrate that you can do the work. Perhaps you have military experience that provides you with experience the government values. In that case, you have a running start, but you still need to build a business.

Construction, Security, Staffing, and Project Management are some of the industries that make for an easier transition from military specialties to government contracting work. You have the skill, experience, training and most importantly...contacts. Those contacts are people who know, like, and trust you already and are willing to help you navigate the Government Contracting (GovCon) landscape. These are the people who want you to do the work because they know they can depend on *you*. Remember, people pay to have their problems solved and they don't want to take chances. They want guarantees. They want peace of mind. They want security. If you create a company based on connections with people who know how good you are at what you do, you have a better chance of getting hired to fill the contract. But if you don't have those relationships, then you have to prove in other ways that you can get the job done.

Government contracting is not kind to companies who are trying to figure out their business model while at the same time trying to figure out the government procurement process. Surely, it has been done, but speaking with those who have succeeded as well as those who have not, the lesson is the same. First make sure your business model is solid enough to expand into the government market.

Personal development is critically important because building a profitable business starts with you...personally. When you open your company, you have no track record. You have no proof that you can or will deliver on your promises. You have no experience to point at and no one who will testify on your behalf. So, it begins with you. Your early customers will not make a purchase because of your product or your service or because they need it and can't find equal or better elsewhere. They will do business with you because they are willing to bet that *you* will fulfill their need and if you can't, that you will make it right. As you deliver consistently on your promises and successfully serve the customers who trust you, you will be able to transfer that trust to your company. You will be able to move from a brand that is representative of you as a person to a brand that is representative of your company as an entity. When that happens, you transition from selling face-to-face to marketing for mass audiences. It all begins with consistently delivering on your promises.

Your personal development program should be framed around the question "How can you make sure you don't fail your customers?" Believe me, people who have been building successful businesses for years still struggle with that equation. In the beginning you are everything and will probably have to do everything, so you need to be crystal clear on your strengths. Are you the visionary, the leader, the operator, the manager, or the developer? To grow your company, you will eventually have to hire people, but until then the workload is on you.

A foundational business principal is...people do business with people they know, like, and trust. Every business deal done and every contract signed is decided by a person. To close a deal, a person signs on the line in some way, shape, or form. The government is no different. In the government, the contracting officer is the person who has the responsibility to match government needs with service providers, so you can establish a competitive advantage by getting a contracting officer to know, like, and trust you.

The government is a bureaucracy, so why would you need a contracting officer to know, like, and trust you? True, a contracting officer cannot just award a contract to you because they like you. However, being liked (in the professional sense) means they see value in *you*. Understand that they don't care about your company or your product or service. They care about having their problem solved and they don't want the problem solver to make more problems for them. They have their clients to serve and they don't want to fail and damage their reputation, so the trust factor is based on them believing that they won't have to worry about you. They want to have confidence that you will not let them down. They want to know that they will get what they paid for and that the price will be fair.

Building relationships with contracting officers is getting to know the people who know the process. Demonstrate your value to them. The benefit of being liked could manifest as guidance on how to prepare and position your company to present well. You will not get insider information, but you can get education on how the system works, so you can prepare your proposals more effectively. Perhaps you didn't know about the importance of responding to a pre-solicitation. You have always waited for the Request for Proposal (RFP) to hit the street. A contracting officer might clarify how participation at an earlier point in the process could mean the difference between getting or losing a contract. It will still be up to you to do the work.

If you are not winning contracts or you are struggling with the contracts you have acquired, go back to basics. Start with the person looking back at you from the mirror every morning. Make sure you are doing what you can to contribute to the success of your company. It all starts with how you prepare. When it comes to preparation, here are some thoughts to help you with your personal development. We'll cover three areas – strengths, purpose, and preparation. Let's begin.

Strengths

Attributes, skills, abilities, knowledge, experience, talent.

Your most important personal insight is knowing what you do best. On a routine basis in business you will face many difficult days. What gets you through is confidence in your ability to overcome whatever obstacles pop up. You will tend to lean on your strengths to solve those challenges and, if you are working from your strengths, your work will feel like play.

In your current condition, you possess a tremendous amount of personal value. You may not be clear on how to deploy that value and, if you are not, that is your most critical task. One of the best ways to gain insight on your capabilities is to take assessments. The Myers Briggs Type Indicator (MBTI) and DiSC profile are widely used, but there are others such as Strength Finders which provide self-awareness and the language to express why you do what you do. You need not embrace everything the assessment reveals. It's a validator of what you already know about yourself but have not previously put into words.

Your background plays a major role in where you decide to invest your energy. My background made it clear to me that strategy and organization are my strengths. I reviewed my personal history to reinforce this revelation. I tracked my decision making through my high school years, my college years and my military career. I focused on how I had applied these talents to achieve my current level of success.

A key element of your strength is an awareness of your weaknesses. Strengths and weaknesses are two sides of the same coin and should not be approached separately. What you do when your back is against the wall is likely to be based on what you trust about yourself…a decision that could lead you to the wrong approach. When all someone has is a hammer, then every problem looks like a nail. If you know your strengths and have high self-awareness, then you will be able to determine when your skill set is inappropriate for the situation. If you are thinking far enough in advance and know the landscape, you can make sure you have a team that has enough skill diversity to cover contingencies. It's also possible that compensation for your weaknesses has led to the development of your current strengths. Understanding both will give you insight into the best role for you in your company.

Just because you are the founder doesn't mean you must be the CEO. Your personality and skill set may make you better suited to be the COO or the CFO. Don't fall victim to the conventional thinking that the founder is automatically the CEO. You can blaze your own trail when it comes to how you position yourself for success. Precedents have been set by founders who have hired a CEO rather than fill the role themselves.

To make sure your weaknesses don't crush you, keep your eyes on your desired outcome. You have to be able to evaluate the problem and determine which resources will best address the issue. This becomes easier when you are strong in purpose. So, let's talk about purpose.

Purpose

Intent, contribution, desired outcome, belief, roadmap, direction.

Every individual has a different perspective on the idea of purpose. In this instance, purpose is expressed as what drives _you_. Perhaps you see government contracting as an easy or acceptable way to make more money. In this case, your purpose is to bring financial stability to your company. After all, the government can be depended on to pay, sometimes even in a timely manner. As long as your team clearly understands that the purpose of doing business with the government is to make sure that you all have jobs, then everyone will be on the same page regarding the mission. This chapter is not about motivation, it's about preparation. Know yourself. Embrace your purpose. Be authentic. A strong stance on your purpose will help you attract the people who arc the best fit.

This company is your baby. You decided that this is how you want to make your living. The drive to make this dream a reality flows from you. No one will work harder than you to make it succeed. Your team will not follow your lead blindly, so your intent must make sense and there has to be something in it for them. You have to make sure they can see what you see…which is why it's called vision. You will attract people who believe what you believe as long as you can communicate it with clarity.

Part of your personal development is to set your intention. If you don't anchor yourself in a desired outcome, then decision making will be haphazard at best. You will compromise where you shouldn't and miss opportunity when it presents itself. Your personal development will shape your preparation, so let's talk about preparation.

Preparation

Certifications, credentials, verification, reputation, community of team and fans.

You have to position yourself to perform. Doing business with the government becomes much easier when you know the rules. The procurement process is complex, but is documented in Federal Acquisition Regulations that can be studied and applied.

The list of certifications and credentials that are offered to people interested in doing business with the government is long. There are some credentials that you must have, such as business licenses and there are some that represent categories such as Service-Disabled Veteran Owned Small Business (SDVOSB). There are programs that establish relationships such as the 8(a) Mentor-Protégé program and there are certifications that indicate skill such as Project Management Professional and Lean Six Sigma.

In preparation, you must think about which of those credentials would be most beneficial to your business. Pursue the credentials that truly tell the story of what you do. Many people chase credentials because they heard that certain types were good to have, but having too many credentials can cause confusion. The reason some people focus on getting credentials is because they want the product to sell itself or they are afraid of missing out on an opportunity. They want to cover so many bases and look so attractive that customers are drawn to them and people with problems will pursue them for solutions. These are not good reasons. A portfolio of credentials could make your business appear to be unfocused, unguided, schizophrenic, and confused. Imagine someone who attempts to dress to appeal to all manner of people. You might see him with a fedora, a Hawaiian shirt, a tie, a suit jacket, short pants, white socks, and wingtip shoes. He would look ridiculous and appeal to no one. Not a good image.

Branding is about presenting the image that represents your persona. In the military each branch of service has a uniform that serves the purpose of the profession. Aviators wear flight suits. They are functional for the mission. Infantry wears battle dress uniforms (BDUs) which are functional for their mission. It would be dangerous and ineffective for infantry to wear a flight suit into combat. The material is wrong. The placement of storage units (pockets) is wrong. It's as wrong as the Hulk wearing an Iron Man suit. Don't dress your business like a two-year old. Think about the message you want potential buyers to get when they perform due diligence on your company. There is nothing wrong with getting every certification in the book. Just make sure those certifications are matched to a solution.

To avoid overextending your company you may want to master one business solution before adding others. That's why it's called business growth. Many businesses start out with a long list of things they think they want to sell to the government in order to cover all bases. They hope it improves their chances to get a contract and if they get one, they scramble to find a way to fulfill that contract. There is nothing wrong with building several business units simultaneously, but it costs money to build them right, so if you have the resources to do it, then go for it. An analogy would be purchasing a piece of property for rent. Until you have a tenant, you are responsible for the mortgage. If you can't keep up with the payments, you lose the house. Your business units are no different. You can hire the staff to run the business unit in anticipation of winning a contract or you can win the contract and then hire the staff. It's one of the great dilemmas facing the business owner. Welcome to the club.

Conclusion

Be thoughtful about your personal development. How you prepare yourself to succeed in the early stages will determine how high you fly when the cage door is opened and you are released into the wild blue yonder.

Here are some steps you can take to do the personal development necessary to succeed in government contracting.

- Assess: Embrace your talent and identify what makes you strong.
- Reflect: Connect your talent to a need or want that the government will pay you to fulfill.
- Educate: Become a professional. Master your craft.
- Certify: Earn and acquire the proof that you have what it takes to perform.
- Sell: Let potential customers know that you are available to make their lives better.

Colonel, US Air Force (retired) Dr. Russ Barnes is Chief Strategist for Systro Solutions, an organization development firm specializing in small business. He has more than 30 years' experience drawn from military service, small business ownership, executive coaching, strategy development and organization design consulting.

His Purposefully Profitable™ Program guides small business owners in creating and implementing a customized progression. In support of the Purposefully Profitable™ Program, he produced the Purposefully Profitable™ Podcast and the Mission Mapping™ Workshop. Russ speaks publically on Organizing Your Business for Profitable Growth and CEO Skills for Small Business. He is the best-selling author of Small Business for Service Members: 15 Things You Need to Know to be Purposefully Profitable and a co-author of two best-selling books: *Game Changers for Government Contractors* and *Mission Unstoppable: Extraordinary Stories of Failures Blessings.*

Dr. Barnes received his Bachelor in Business Administration from Manhattan College (NY), his Master in Business Administration (MBA) from Embry-Riddle Aeronautical University, his Master of Science in Strategic Studies from Air University, and his PhD in Organization Development from Benedictine University. The title of his dissertation is Organization Design for Small Business: A Discovery of Business Fundamentals for Executing a Purposeful Path to Profitability.

Connect with Russ by email - russ@systro.org or LinkedIn (www.linkedin.com/in/rcbarnes).

For more information and education from Systro Solutions visit: https://www.systro.org/purposefully-profitable-program

Chapter 2.
12 Common Challenges for New Government Contractors

By Joshua Frank

Managing Partner, RSM Federal

Having trained thousands of companies, to take a quote from Farmers Insurance, "I know a thing or two, because I've seen a thing or two," I often tell companies it's not rocket science. Successfully selling to federal agencies and the Department of Defense requires education and most important, *strategies for executing what you've learned.*

For those new to Public Sector, what we call the government market, it can be overwhelming. But if you learn the tactics and strategies to be successful, it can be a very lucrative endeavor.

In that vein, I want to share the twelve most common challenges and questions that companies face when they first enter the government market. In fact, many of these remain a challenge for more established companies. There are quite a few misconceptions on what you should or should not do to be successful in government sales. I want to set (or realign) your expectations so that you don't make the same mistakes. This will help accelerate your corporate strategy and get your business development off to the right start.

1. Realistic Expectations

Let's start with expectations. More specifically, setting accurate expectations. When you first enter the government market, you are likely to receive guidance and recommendations from dozens of organizations, colleagues, and consultants. You have your choice of free help and paid coaching. Most companies start with free services. While I don't have a formal relationship with the Association of Procurement Technical Assistance Centers (APTAC), I do work with many of them and their clients. They are a free service funded by the Department of Defense and your local university. This is the most common starting point. There is likely a PTAC office where you live.

Back to expectations. Let's start with the first one. Government sales is a long-game. It's strategic. The decision to enter the government market requires that you create a strategy and spend months putting it in place. **There are no shortcuts**. If your commercial sales are down and you want government revenue to offset your lack of commercial sales, you will likely be disappointed. The average company takes eighteen to twenty-four months to successfully generate a government revenue stream. However, you can do it in six to twelve months if you develop and put in place the right tactics and strategies. That's my expertise – the tactics and strategies required to apply what you've learned to accelerate revenue.

Deciding to go after government sales is not a tactical decision. This is the most important of the challenges that I help companies manage. So, if you are desperate for cash flow, *focus on your commercial sales*. While focusing on commercial sales, start educating yourself on how successful companies win government contracts.

For those just dipping their toes into the world of government sales, or those already swimming but need a hand, two recommendations. First, you need the right mindset. Second, you need the right tools. Let's discuss.

For your mindset - another book. *An Insider's Guide to Winning Government Contracts - Real World Strategies, Lessons, and Recommendations*. An Amazon #1 bestseller, it is one of the most valuable resources for understanding how to approach the market. Of all the resources I've developed over the years, it is the most valuable for entering the market. I put a link to the book at the end of this chapter.

For the right tools – register for an account on the Federal Access (FA) platform. Federal Access provides all the tactics, strategies, training videos, and templates you need for prospecting, business development, teaming, writing proposals, and back-office operations. You will find a link at the end of the chapter on how to join the 1,000 companies that use these resources.

These two resources will help you tackle the long-game and give you the tools you need to be successful.

2. The Capability Statement

I don't want to reinvent the wheel. For many that read this book, the capability statement is one of the first resources they are told they need for government sales.

What is a capability statement? Simply, it's a one-page marketing slick for government buyers, small business offices, and your teaming partners.

What's the objective? Your capability statement should communicate your value; *not simply the products or services you sell; and not focused on your socio-economic certifications*.

Okay. This is when we need to take a step back and level-set. One of the greatest challenges you will face is bridging business strategy with government sales strategy.

I don't care if you have a business degree or a high school education. You cannot successfully sell to the government (or for that matter, the commercial market) without thinking like a business professional.

More than fifty percent of companies fail to win government contracts. Why? Because they act like robots, doing only what they are told to do. Call the small business office; bring a copy of your capability statement to every meeting; immediately tell the government and teaming partners that you are a Woman-Owned Small Business (WOSB), 8(a), HUBZone, or Service Disabled Veteran Owned Small Business (SDVOSB). Don't simply do what others tell you to do. Think from a business perspective. Trust your gut!

Your capability statement is intended to prove (or create the perception) that your company is very good at what you do. "Very good" is defined as having experience; providing solid value to your customers; and that you have a mature business. You can still define your company as experienced and providing value even if you are an entrepreneur or very small business. **It's the strategies you use to facilitate the right perceptions**. That's all a capability statement provides, a perception of competence and value. That's why a capability statement is nothing more than a one-page marketing brochure.

If all you do is list your products or services, your DUNS / SAMMI number, the awards you've received, and an introductory write-up on your company, you're not starting-off on the right foot.

Your focus is communicating value. That requires *quantifiable* and *qualifiable metrics, numbers and percentages.*

There is a six-second rule on capability statements. The average person will only spend six seconds looking at your capability statement. The average government buyer or teaming partner has no idea who you are. They really don't care. You are one of hundreds of companies that sell what you sell. They are busy. They are focused on their own requirements. You have six seconds for them to quickly look-down at your capability statement and have them think, "Okay! This company looks like they know what they're doing."

Six seconds. You need strong value. You need customer graphics to prove past performance… in six seconds.

And that brings us to challenge number three.

3. Communicating Your Value

Until you can successfully communicate the value of your products and services, you're minimizing the value of your time when updating your website, creating a capability statement, giving your elevator-pitch, and writing bids or proposals.

Let's stop for a moment. ***Read the previous paragraph again.*** To be clear, if you want to be perceived as a mature and competent company, everything hinges on your ability to communicate the value of your solutions. It's that simple…and that complex.

At this point, many readers are thinking, "Yea, yea, yea…I know the value my products or services provide." However, from having trained thousands of companies I can tell you that it's often more than you think.

This topic, this challenge, is so important, that I'll use a case study.

In California, there is a company called International Unified Technologies (IUT). In business for only three years, they have built a $2.7-million-dollar business helping local companies deploy wireless networks.

At $2.7 million, their margins are fairly average and their back-office has grown from two to six employees.

IUT has successfully completed seven commercial contracts - three with local universities, two with local hospitals, and two with fairly large corporations.

When I first started working with them, I asked, "So, what do you do?" What am I looking for in their answer? *I'm looking for value.*

They responded with, "We are a woman-owned small business (WOSB) information technology (IT) company that develops and installs wireless networks. We've deployed wireless networks for various hospitals, universities, and corporations. We're a growing company and we've successfully deployed seven networks in the last several years."

Hmmm. That's not a bad start. I clearly know they are a WOSB; they are a technology company; and they've deployed seven networks over the last several years."

But there is one problem. As a perspective customer, they are *no different than the other fifty companies that have reached out to me.*

There is no perception that they are really that great at what they do. So what if they have seven contracts? Their competition has seven or more. So what if they work with universities and hospitals? Their competition has similar past performance!

Almost every company I've coached started in this manner. *It's normal.* So I walked IUT through competency-mapping, a process to better understanding their company's value. When we were done, this is how they described what their company provides:

"Josh, we're in the business of helping companies and organizations extend their connectivity and speed of access across the enterprise. Over the last three years, we've deployed wireless networks for 7 organizations supporting more than 55,000 employees, geographically dispersed across 37 buildings, in 12 different cities. On average, our designs have increased speed of access to core systems by 13% and decreased customer complaints by 41%. Our clients include the third largest hospital system on the West Coast, a Fortune 500 company, and an NCAA Division 1 school."

Don't simply tell me what you sell! That's not communicating value. You need quantifiable and qualifiable metrics.

Also, notice that on the second go-around *they did not mention they were a Woman-Owned Small Business (WOSB)*. Why? **Because that's not the value they provide**.

Remember when I said you have to bridge business strategy with government sales strategy? When you jump out the gate with WOSB, what are you telling me? You're telling me that you believe the value of your company is that you are woman-owned. Think about that.

That's. Not. Your. Value. Your value is the value that your products and services provide to your customers.

How can you possibly create a strong and compelling website, capability statement, bid, or proposal... if you don't know how to communicate your value?

For those of you that need help on communicating value, I provide step-by-step strategies on mapping your past performance (experience and past contracts) through various webinars, in Federal Access, and in Amazon's *An Insider's Guide to Winning Government Contracts*.

4. Your Core Products or Services

Communicating what you sell and what you're really good at is a challenge for small and large businesses alike... but especially for small businesses. For many entrepreneurs and small business owners, they think their business will focus on one solution to only shift direction after they've won one or two major contracts.

"Oh! We thought we were a software development company! But we just won two contracts, as a subcontractor to Northrup Grumman and SAIC, for providing network engineering services. So... now we're a network engineering company!"

First, there's nothing wrong with this. Nothing wrong with going where the money is. But you didn't say, "Yea...we're good at software development (that's what you did for ten years before you started the company), but let's focus on doing something we've never done before."

When you look at this company's hypothetical website, they list the following services:

- software development
- database administration
- wireless networking
- project management
- engineering services
- record's management
- call center / help desk operations
- cyber security
- data management; and
- product reseller

But, what is their core service? They list help desk operations, cyber security, software development, and being a reseller for products. It is highly unlikely that a small business would have all of these as core competencies. (It's possible but for this discussion, let's assume this is not the case).

There is nothing wrong with having all of these services on your website or having the NAICS codes for these services listed in SAM. But operating in this manner is simply targets of opportunity. You need to say to yourself, "Yes, we can do all these things. We may even have past performance on most of them, but what are the two or three services we will strategically position for in the coming year?"

If you don't ask this question and you don't focus on the answer, you will come across on your website, on your capability statement, and in verbal discussions as a "jack of all trades" who really doesn't know what they do. This applies to government buyers and teaming partners. This is very common with smaller companies.

5. Pre-Acquisition vs Acquisition
Strategic vs Tactical

99% of companies that first enter the government market laser-focus on activities in the acquisition phase. While you may tactically win one or two contracts, you will not consistently win contracts unless you focus your business development activities in the *pre-acquisition* phase.

Pre-acquisition is before the government releases a bid or solicitation. That means you won't learn about the opportunity in DLA's Internet Bid Board System (DIBBS), beta.SAM's contract opportunities, GSA eBuy's portal, or any other government contract management system. However, there are a couple exceptions which are 1) sources sought and requests for information and 2) pre and draft solicitations. A sources sought is a market research tool where the government is attempting to validate if there are two or more small businesses that can do the work. Requests for information are often for products or services that buyer has not purchased before. Draft solicitations are also pre-acquisition because you can't submit a bid or proposal yet.

Pre-acquisition is engaging your **three annual targets** (these are not opportunities but the agencies and / or military commands that buy most of what you sell). You engage pre-acquisition by calling the small business offices, attending conferences and events where you know government buyers are attending, and through the time-tested effort of picking up the phone and calling until you get someone to pick up.

Pre-acquisition is strategic. It's positioning your company in the market so that you know about opportunities *before they are released to the public*. You aren't focused on engaging opportunities. You are engaging buyers. You engage agencies and military commands that have purchased the most of what you sell over the last three to five years.

The acquisition phase starts when a requirement is released for bid. This includes DIBBS opportunities and beta.SAM solicitations.

The acquisition phase is tactical. You are *reactive* with little ability to collect intelligence or market information that will make you more competitive than the competition.

If you need help with tactics and strategies for acquisition and pre-acquisition, a good starting point is *An Insider's Guide to Winning Government Contracts* (on Amazon - full of strategies for helping you position in the market.)

6. Bid-Matching & Contract Management Tools

There are more than 1,000 systems you can pay for to help you identify opportunities to bid on. They are called different names: bid-matching systems, contract management systems, and market intelligence tools. Of these, there are a dozen that are commonly referred to and used by our clients. And then there are two or three that I would recommend based on what you sell.

As much as you probably want me to identify these systems, I won't. There are both business and political reasons for this. One key reason is what happens when one of these tools stops providing the level of value they need to provide? Then I'm quoted in this and other books recommending a tool that no longer provides the necessary value. I've already fallen into this trap once. If you want recommendations, just connect with me on LinkedIn and ask me!

Most companies, small and large, that use these tools to find opportunities, *don't win many contracts*. Now you're asking, "What? No, that can't be true. Every company we know, that targets the government, has one of these bid-match systems." And you would be correct on the latter point. Almost every company has one. They either have a free one provided by their local Procurement Technical Assistance Center (PTAC) or a paid one. *But most are not winning contracts.*

Why? Because bid-matching / contract management systems are *primarily used during the acquisition phase*. Yes, many of the larger systems market a focus on recompete contracts and market intelligence. All of this is important and can help you. But remember what we learned in the prior section on pre-acquisition versus acquisition.

Most companies use bid-matching / contract management systems to support "Acquisition" activities. They use these systems to find and bid on contracts. Nothing wrong with that! It's a key purpose of the system.

However, because many companies use these tools as their primary sales tool, as the primary sales strategy, and don't understand that 80% of your business development effort should be in pre-acquisition, most of these companies don't win contracts.

Finding Opportunities Is The Easy Part
You don't win government contracts because you find the right opportunities. You win because you understand how to position for those opportunities.

Here's what you need to remember. If you don't have a strong business development strategy that is focused on pre-acquisition, these systems will not provide the value you expect. In fact, they'll make you feel like you're doing all the right things only to find a year later, scratching your head, wondering why you haven't won anything.

Never spend money on one of these systems unless you've identified 'propensity' for who buys what you sell, how much, and how often; unless you've identified your three strategic annual targets; unless you have started to build a strong teaming strategy; and you understand the tactics and strategies for influencing government procurements.

Trust your gut! You know what I'm saying makes sense. Don't spend money on these systems *until you're ready to take advantage of them*.

7. Competitive Price Point (CPP)

There are many definitions for "Competitive Price Point (CPP)." It is simply the price required to win a bid.

Simple huh? Not so much. At a macro-level, it really is that simple. Your pricing is low enough to win but high enough to generate profit. At a micro-level, it's developing a process to calculate the labor rates on each labor category or the pricing for a product.

One of the challenges companies face when they enter the federal market is figuring out what to charge. Unlike the private sector (corporate America), the government publishes extensive data on past contracts. The government also publishes extensive data on other company's labor rates and product pricing.

You just need to know where to look!

If you sell services, you can start getting an idea on what your competition is charging via the following sites:

- GSA CALC - https://calc.gsa.gov/
- GSA eLibary - https://www.gsaelibrary.gsa.gov/ElibMain/home.do
- USASpending.gov - https://www.usaspending.gov/ ; and
- beta.SAM - https://beta.sam.gov/

If you sell products, you can start with the following sites:

- GSA Advantage - https://www.gsaadvantage.gov/
- DIBBS - https://www.dibbs.bsm.dla.mil/
- beta.SAM - https://beta.sam.gov/

However, nothing is ever simple. For example, because the General Services Administration (GSA) negotiates labor rates and product pricing with companies getting a GSA Schedule, the negotiation often results in companies having similar rates and pricing. What's important to recognize is that because of this, *most companies don't use their GSA Schedule labor rates.* They often bid three to five points below their published rates. Highlight this. If you see a labor rate of $35.00 per hour, I would immediately assume they are bidding $33.25 to $33.95 (3%-5%). Of course, I'll also lookup their contracts in beta.SAM's Data Bank and attempt to validate the pricing.

There's no right or wrong on this. You truly learn how competitive your rates are when you win or lose. But from a business perspective you need to identify the competitive price point for each opportunity you bid.

It makes you more competitive.

It increases your bid or proposal win rate (PWIN). Wouldn't you prefer to win three out of every seven bids versus one out of every seven?

Now, you might look at a competitor's labor rate and say, "No way. There's no way this labor rate will work for us! It leaves zilch for profit." If this happens to you, we need to look at your fully burdened rate.

Imagine two companies sell the exact same service and are the same size. One company operates out of a 1,000 square foot office and the other out of a 5,000 square foot office. Immediately we know one company likely has more overhead than the other. If all things were equal, the company with less overhead, paying less for office space, can / might have more competitive pricing.

My point is that just because two companies sell the same product or service does not mean they will have the same rates. They have different levels of overhead, G&A, expenses.

I've coached a lot of companies. But now and then I have to say:

> *"You are not going to be competitive in the government market due to your pricing. Unless you decrease your overhead and other costs, you'll never be able to **consistently win** with enough profit to make it viable."*

There are many websites and resources you can use to figure out what your competition is charging. But make sure you are controlling your costs or you'll find that achieving a Competitive Price Point will be an uphill battle. See?

8. Socio-Economic Statuses

If you have ever heard me present at national events, you've heard my business approach to socio-economic status:

> *Your status is a balancing differentiator. You are not going to win a contract because you are woman-owned, minority-owned, or veteran-owned.*
>
> ***The value of your company is not your status!***
>
> *The value of your company is the value of the products or services **you provide to your customers.***

Too many companies believe that their status will win them a contract. This is drilled into the minds of small business owners by many non-profit organizations, paid consultants, and government buyers.

You need to stop thinking that your certification is a key part to winning contracts.

It's not.

Yes, 23% of all government spend is supposed to be set-aside for small business. Yes, there are mandated spend percentages for woman-owned (WOSB - 5%), minority and socially disadvantaged (8a - 5%), service disabled veteran owned (SDVOSB - 3%), and HUBZone (3%) to name the big ones.

But I'll ask a question that I often use when coaching companies just like yours: "If the Department of Labor releases an opportunity that is set-aside for woman-owned small business (WOSB) and 17 companies respond to the solicitation, what is the value of your WOSB certification?"

What do all 17 companies have in common? Yes, they are all WOSB. Each of these companies submit a proposal and all are in source selection. So I'll ask the question again, "What value does their WOSB status provide them?"

That's right – *nothing*.

Now, I don't want you thinking I'm Mr. Negative when it comes to certifications. Two weeks after opening a new B2G operating division, my company won an $82,000 SDVOSB set-aside contract with the Department of Veterans Affairs. There's no way we would have won the contract without having the SDVOSB certification.

Socio-economic statuses and their certifications decrease the number of competitors. This is really important and very valuable.

However, I want you to think differently about your status. Yes, it is a differentiator. Yes, it will open doors. But it is what I call a *"Balancing Differentiator"* because once you're in source selection, if you don't communicate the value of your products or services, your status will provide no value and you are unlikely to win the opportunity.

If after reading this chapter you say, "Wow! I get it!" then you will have successfully looked at your status from a business perspective and not a government sales perspective.

You will not win contracts because you are certified. You will win contracts because you communicate the value of what you sell.

This is not semantics. It's understanding how to bridge government sales strategy with business strategy.

9. Professional Associations

One of the three core business development activities to consistently winning government contracts is having a strong programmatic teaming strategy.

Do you have the right number of teaming partners? The answer is different for every company depending on what you sell and your industry.

Professional associations are critical to your success. Not every industry has an association but many do. Joining an association provides you with the following value:

- opportunity to learn from other government contractors
- opportunity to build relationships with successful contractors where you can start priming and subcontracting
- access to local, regional, and national webinars, seminars, conferences, and events; and
- access to government decision makers, buyers, and champions

I'm always telling my clients to get out from behind their computer. A focus on pre-acquisition sales strategies requires you do just that!

Here are some of the major associations for government contractors. Just because you don't see your industry listed doesn't mean there isn't one.

- Armed Forces Communications and Electronics Association (AFCEA) - for technology, electronics, and communications https://www.afcea.org/
- National Defense Industrial Association (NDIA) - supporting strategic dialogue in national security; includes technology, cybersecurity, ammunition, and many other industries that impact national security. https://www.ndia.org/
- Society of American Military Engineers (SAME) – for the AEC community supporting architecture, engineering, and construction. https://www.same.org/

If you don't see an association for your industry, talk to government contractors in your industry and ask them. There are many others.

10. Using beta.SAM's Three Core Capabilities

Where do I find opportunities? Where can I find how much the government paid for this contract three years ago? Where can I find companies I can subcontract to that have won contracts *at this exact location,* in the *last five years,* with annual revenue of *at least $5 million,* that is also SBA *8a certified?* You get the idea and yes, all of this information is publicly available!

If you have used beta.SAM and you're still trying to figure out how to use it, you're not alone. beta.SAM is part of the new Integrated Award Environment (IAW). More than half a dozen government systems have been shut-down and migrated into IAW. beta.SAM is one of the them.

SAM stands for the "System for Award Management." beta.SAM replaced FedBizOpps (FBO).

Even though beta.SAM is fairly new, it's not hard learning how to use it. Like anything else, it just takes someone showing you how to do it!

There are more than a dozen capabilities and tools in beta.SAM. There are three that companies must learn to use for government sales. They are:

1) **Contract Opportunities**; how to search and how to save automatic queries so you get opportunities via email.
2) **Entity Information**; how to lookup competitors and potential teaming partners and using this information as part of your sales and teaming strategies.
3) **Data Bank**; how to lookup information to answer almost any question on historical contract data, pricing, names of companies that won contracts, the contracting office spending the money, and more than 200 other data points!

I've included training videos on how to setup beta.SAM to search for opportunities (20 minute video); and how to setup beta.SAM's Data Bank (1.5 hour video) for advanced search and business intelligence. Included with these videos are the documents that provide the fields you need to use and other best practices.

To access these training videos and EVERY resource that RSM Federal provides to its clients, simply register for an account on the Federal Access Platform. https://federal-access.com/govconexpertsbook.

11. Teaming = Success

Did you know that 90% of small businesses get their first several contracts as a subcontractor? They don't sign a contract with the government. They sign a Teaming Agreement (TA) with a Prime contractor (who wins and signs a contract with the government).

To reiterate, a strong teaming strategy is one of the three core sales activities you must perform to *consistently win government contracts.*

Most companies use a hybrid sales approach with both direct and indirect sales. This is just another way of saying priming and subcontracting. Not every company, because of the products or services they sell, will necessarily require a subcontracting strategy. But since 99% of companies can generate revenue via subcontracting, you can be fairly sure that your company likely needs a teaming strategy built into your overall business development strategy.

What's the value? First, subcontractors normally don't have to write and submit the bid or proposal. That's awesome for companies new to government sales! You get to watch another company go through the proposal process and you get to learn how they do it! This is why most companies start as subcontractors.

Last, I want to clarify one of the most common questions raised by new contractors. "Does working as a subcontractor count as past performance?"

Absolutely. As does your commercial past performance.

When you're ready to be a Prime, your past performance on subcontracts becomes your core past performance when you bid.

I could write an entire book on teaming and most of my tactics and strategies are in Federal Access (link at end of chapter). For companies just starting in the government market, make sure that your sales strategy includes both prime and subcontracting.

I often recommend that companies just starting out use the percentage of 30/70 or 40/60, the number of opportunities in your pipeline that are prime versus subcontracting.

12. Too Many Websites!

The General Services Administration (GSA) has streamlined many of the government's various websites over the last several years. I'm often asked, how many different websites do you use for government sales? The answer is about fifty with a half-dozen that I use on a fairly regular basis.

Many companies stumble around until they figure out which sites provide the most value, as well as what you should use each site for.

Here are the core websites that my company and our clients use:

- **beta.SAM** for opportunity search, finding teaming partners, and historical contract data. https://beta.sam.gov/
- **DLA's Internet Bid Board System (DIBBS)** for finding opportunities for product sales and competitive pricing. https://www.dibbs.bsm.dla.mil/
- **Contract Awarded Labor Category (CALC) Tool** for finding every labor rate, by labor category, for every company on one of the 19 major contract vehicles. https://calc.gsa.gov/
- **GSA Advantage** for what your competition is charging for their products. https://www.gsaadvantage.gov/
- **GSA eLibrary** for the complete pricing list for services (some product) for companies that have a GSA Schedule contract vehicle. https://www.gsaelibrary.gsa.gov/

There are many other websites for agency and military procurement forecasts; NAICS, PSC, FSC, CAGE, and other codes; websites for working with the various agencies and commands; sites for contract data on awarded contracts; and much more. I developed an Internet bookmark file that you can upload directly into your browser and you'll have access to all of the sites! It's in Federal Access.

So, that's twelve of the common challenges and issues that small businesses face when they enter the government market.

Which of these twelve hit closest to home? Which of these tactics and recommendations will you add to your sales strategy?

Something to think about.

If you want to learn more of Joshua's tactics and strategies, several recommendations:

- **Coaching** to accelerate your business today in federal contracting contact the RSM Federal team using the link below: https://rsmfederal.com/contact/

- Amazon #1 bestseller *An Insider's Guide to Winning Government Contracts* https://bit.ly/GovConInsidersGuide

- Amazon #1 bestseller *Game Changers for Government Contractors* https://bit.ly/GovConGameChangers

- *The Government Sales Manual* https://bit.ly/GovConSalesManual

- Free *Podcast Game Changers for Government Contractors* where we interview many of the industry's top GovCon experts https://bit.ly/GovConPodcast

---

Federal Access Platform for GovCon
Get more than 300 essential documents and templates, 100+ training videos, and industry leading Subject Matter Expertise (SME) to accelerate your government sales. You can start your journey with us today for $29 by visiting https://federal-access.com/govconexpertsbook

---

***

Award-winning business coach, professional speaker, and bestselling author, Mr. Frank is a nationally recognized authority on government sales and business acceleration. With 30 years in the government market, he speaks nationally on federal acquisition and business strategy.

He specializes in the development and implementation of tactics and strategies required to differentiate, position for, and win government contracts. Referred to as the *Professor of Government Sales*, his training sessions, highly educational and thought-provoking, are consistently rated the top sessions at national conferences and events.

He has more than 30 years' experience drawn from military service, small business ownership, executive coaching, strategy development and organization design consulting.

Managing Partner at RSM Federal, Mr. Frank is author of Amazon's blockbuster and #1 bestseller *An Insider's Guide to Winning Government Contracts – Real World Strategies, Lessons, and Recommendations*, the highest selling book on Amazon today.

Mr. Frank was awarded Veteran Business of the Year by the SBA and Industry Small Business Advocate of the Year by SAME. A former military intelligence officer, Masters in Management Information Systems (MIS) and a Master's in Business Administration (MBA). Connect on LinkedIn https://www.linkedin.com/in/joshuapfrank

Chapter 3.
Propelling Your Company Onward in Government Contracting

By Emily Harman

Founder of The Onward Movement, President of Emily Harman Coaching and Consulting

The day I retired from the Department of the Navy as the Director of the Office of Small Business Programs, I published the first seven episodes of the Onward Podcast. (https://emilyharman.com/onwardpodcast/). Over the course of the next year, I interviewed hundreds of Onward Podcast guests on how they moved forward in the face of adversity.

I've noticed three key themes addressed by every one of my guests: 1) Know where you are and where you're going; 2) Ask for help; and 3) Be persistent. These themes also apply to Government Contracting (GovCon). Let's face it, contracting with the federal government can be intimidating and the points made by my guests in addressing and overcoming adversity apply to government contracting.

Most likely, there are hundreds of companies in government contracting that sell the same product or service as you. Following these three tips will help your company stand out amongst the competition.

Government contracting can be a dry topic so I include examples from Onward Podcast episodes throughout this chapter to drive my points home.

Know Where You Are and Where You're Going

It seems simple enough: know where you are and where you are going. I can't tell you how many small business owners don't know where they're going. They may think they know but their actions speak louder than their words. They're impatient and go after any and every opportunity that comes their way hoping that something will stick. This is exhausting and typically doesn't result in the desired outcome - winning a government contract.

As a small business owner, you have to be clear on your purpose. Nothing helps you get more clear than writing your ideas down. Write your business plan and develop a written strategy to keep you on track. You will encounter daily distractions along the way. Refer to your strategy often, sometimes daily, to stay focused and on the right path.

Dr. Russ Barnes, author of *Your Amazing Itty Bitty Small Business for Service Members Book*, describes strategy as "how to get from where you are to where you want to be." Once you've decided on where you want to be you can assess where you are and begin to connect the dots.

Of course, there are several steps along your path from Point A to Point B. As you progress and the environment changes around you, you will need to adapt. Once you establish your Point B, create a roadmap that enables you to see different steps that sit between your Point A and Point B.

Dr. Barnes uses a common example to illustrate this point. When planning a vacation, you start with where you want to spend your holiday. Then you map your journey to that destination. If you decide to drive, you may encounter road work and detours, mechanical failures, bad weather or other unanticipated obstacles. You adjust your course and reorient yourself toward the preset destination. It's no different in business.

There will be many ways to get to your point B. Having a well thought out strategy will give you structure and an ability to measure your progress along the way. It also helps you get really clear on where you want to go, why you want to go there, and how you will get there. Be prepared to be flexible and make adjustments along the way. Working with a coach or someone who successfully navigated a similar path can give you confidence and save you time.

Let's take a detour. Fifteen-year-old Rodney Flowers knew exactly where he was as he lay in the hospital bed (Point A). Rodney explained, "A team of neurologists visited my bedside to pass along my diagnosis. My diagnosis was quadriplegic. I was completely paralyzed. I had no movement or sensation in any of my extremities. And the doctor said I had a 92% chance of remaining that way for the rest of my life."

Rodney knew this was his Point A and it was not going to be his Point B. Rodney says in his Onward Podcast interview, "I developed a strong belief in God. I started looking at what is possible, and that was really the game-changing element of all of this: *what is possible?* Because you want to recover. You want to walk again. You want to live the life that you had."

The majority of Rodney's battle was mental, not physical, and the lessons learned from his story can be applied to government contracting. Think about what you *can* do and focus on that. Don't fixate on what you can't do. He also practiced what he *could do* over and over again. For government contractors, this means, setting a strategy to get from Point A to Point B and *executing that strategy with determination.*

By the way, Rodney is walking. He reached his Point B.

Focus on the strengths of your company; respond to Sources Sought; meet with potential clients; respond to Requests for Proposals in the areas of your company's strengths. Do this over and over again. Ask for and listen to feedback when you aren't successful. Adjust and keep going.

The GovCon Small Business Growth Model developed by Solvability and addressed in Chapter 7 of the Amazon #1 bestseller _Game Changers for Government Contractors,_ is a great place to start as you develop your company's strategy - https://bit.ly/GovConGameChangers.

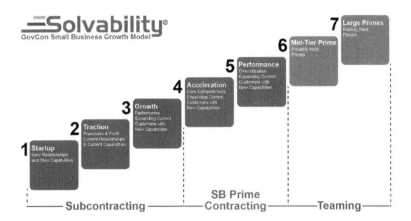

=Solvability®
GovCon Small Business Growth Model

1 Startup
New Relationships
and New Capabilities

2 Traction
Processes & Profit
Current Relationships
& Current Capabilities

3 Growth
Performance
Expanding Current
Customers with
New Capabilities

4 Acceleration
Core Competencies
Expanding Current
Customers with
New Capabilities

5 Performance
Diversification
Expanding Current
Customers with
New Capabilities

6 Mid-Tier Prime
Privately Held
Primes

7 Large Primes
Publicly Held
Primes

Subcontracting ———— SB Prime Contracting ———— Teaming

I've seen many small business owners want to immediately start at steps 4 or 5. I don't recommend this approach unless you are selling something so unique that your government customer is unable to procure it from anyone but your company (which is a rare situation.) While every small business owner believes their product or service is unique, the uniqueness needs to be determined by the government customer, not you.

Study the GovCon Small Business Growth Model. Once you identify where your company is in the model, learn what you need to do to move to the next level of growth. Make sure you focus on the fundamentals and check out Chapter 5, The Basic Fundamentals of Business in the book _Game Changers for Government Contractors_.

The GovCon Small Business Growth Model is a framework for understanding the requirements for each stage of growth. There are options for scaling your business and you may find your business moves back and forth between different stages, which is perfectly normal.

Achieving the next level in the growth model creates a new set of challenges. That's why it's important to work with a coach. Check out Chapter 33 in _Game Changers for Government Contractors_ to learn the top 10 reasons why you need a coach. Successful GovCon Small Business owners work with coaches and listen to advice. They don't go it alone. That's why the theme "Ask for Help" is next. But before we head to the second theme, let's take another detour. I'd like to highlight one more Onward Podcast guest's journey from Point A to Point B.

My Naval Academy roommate's daughter, Clara Brown was an avid athlete as a competitive gymnast, runner, and skier before sustaining an incomplete spinal cord injury at the C5/C6 level...at age 12 (https://en.wikipedia.org/wiki/Clara_Brown_(cyclist). Clara moved to the Shepherd Center in Atlanta, where they specialize in spinal cord and brain injury rehabilitation, and it was there that she began to get some feeling and function back. She started walking on the treadmill and made great progress.

A few months later Clara began experiencing excruciating pain in her left leg and was diagnosed with avascular necrosis, which was cutting off the blood supply and causing her bone to die. Listen to this Onward Podcast episode and learn about Clara's amazing journey from Point A to Point B. Follow Clara as she races towards the Paralympics in Tokyo as a member of the U.S. Paralympic Cycling Team. You can listen to Clara's episode here: https://emilyharman.com/podcasts/racing-toward-tokyo-with-clara-brown/

Ask for Help

As a small business owner in the Federal Market space, you can't possibly know it all! Just to make my point, how many of these *common* acronyms are familiar to you?

COR, CMMC, SBIR, CAS, PIA, IDIQ, COTS, FAR, DFARS, DUNS, NAICS, BIC, OTA, SBSA, SAM, DCMA, GSA, NMCARS, SBA, 8(a), WOSB, EDWOSB, SDVOSB, WAWF, RFP, RFQ, LPTA, CPARS, GWAC, PPQ, KPI, STTR, JV, CFR, PTAC, SBDC, SOW, SOO, OSDBU, OSBP, FFP, CPFF, CPIF, CPAF, BOA...the list goes on and on.

Successful small business owners ask for help. The good news is there are numerous free or low cost Federal contracting resources.

- Small Business Administration (SBA)
- Procurement Technical Assistance Centers (PTAC)
- Small Business Development Centers (SBDC)
- Community Banks
- Economic Development Organizations
- Service Corps of Retired Executives (SCORE)
- Defense Contract Audit Agency (DCAA)

- Office of Small Business Programs (OSBP) for the Department of Defense (DoD)
- Office of Small and Disadvantaged Business Utilization for non DoD Agencies
- Minority Business Development Agency
- Where in Federal Contracting website
- Government Contracting related podcasts
- Industry Organizations
    - National Defense Industrial Association (NDIA)
    - Armed Forces Communications Electronics Association (AFCEA)
    - Women in Defense (WID)
    - National Contract Management Association (NCMA)
    - Association of the U.S. Army (AUSA)
    - Navy League
    - And many more

It's not easy to ask for help. Asking for help means giving control to someone else. It may make you feel as if you're coming across as incompetent. But keep in mind that the reason all of these organizations were established is because GovCon is not easy. They're here to help you.

Let's take a detour: Steven Iselin, a retired U.S. Navy Commander and retired Principal Deputy Assistant Secretary of the Navy for Energy, Installations, and Environment asked for help. In his Onward Podcast episode, Ways to Cope with Mental Wellness, Steve shares how depression made him go from feeling like he had it all to being suicidal within weeks.

Ultimately, Steve asked for help and learned how to live with depression. In this interview he shares strategies and resources he used to improve his mental wellness. Steve says "When you are in the middle of a depression, you struggle with sleeping and you struggle with eating. Everything gets thrown off." You can listen to Steve's Onward Podcast episode here: https://emilyharman.com/podcasts/surviving-depression-and-moving-onward-with-steve-iselin/

Steve not only sought help, he listened and took the advice of his mentors and counselors. To be successful in GovCon, you've got to be able to listen and take advice. There are plenty of small business owners in the GovCon space who don't do this and it's obvious by what they say, the actions they take, and the disappointing outcomes they experience.

If you've exhausted the use of free or minimal cost resources and still need help, there are other options. To be honest, when I worked for the Department of the Navy as the Director of the Office of Small Business Programs, I didn't fully understand the value brought by GovCon coaches. Now, I see it.

The free/minimal resources as well as the government Small Business Professionals are not staffed or authorized to perform the duties of a coach. For example, as a government employee, my focus was not how to grow *your* specific small business. It was to provide a fair opportunity for all small businesses to compete for government contracts.

There's a difference…a BIG difference.

Check out Chapter 33 of book *Game Changers for Government Contractors* https://bit.ly/GovConGameChangers to learn the top 10 reasons why you need a coach. Successful GovCon Small Business owners work with coaches and listen to their advice. Consider establishing your own personal board of directors as recommended by Onward Podcast guest Angie Swartz. Angie is a life, business, and career coach, and the founder of Life Purpose Advisor. You can hear tips on how to select your board members by listening to her episode here: https://emilyharman.com/podcasts/create-your-own-personal-board-of-directors/

Be Persistent (Laser focused)

Doing business in Federal Market takes persistence. It's a long sales cycle - 18-24 months. As a small business owner, you've got to be laser focused and persistent to get from Point A to Point B.

Persistence paid off for Onward Podcast guest Lisa Spector. A Juilliard trained pianist who plays the piano for a living, Lisa suffered a bad fall in June of 2017 that shattered her right hand. After three surgeries for seven complicated fractures, she dove into music with only her left hand. Now, after her 4th surgery and numerous hours of physical therapy, Lisa can play again with both hands.

Lisa sought help *and* she did the work required to get better, day in and day out. She didn't let distractions get in her way. You can learn more about Lisa's journey in this Onward Podcast episode:

As a small business owner doing business in the Federal Market, this is exactly what you need to do. Keep your eye on Point B and don't get distracted. There may be times when you need to pivot. Something could cause you to adjust your Point B. However, make sure you pivot or adjust consciously and for a good reason. Listen to your coaches.

It's not by accident that the word "persistence" shows up in Episode 1 of the book _Game Changers for Government Contractors_. Author Michael LeJeune writes "How many phone calls does it take to win a contract? As many as it takes…" "How long does it take to win a contract? As long as it takes…" Per Michael, (and he is 100% correct), you will also be told "no" or "not at this time" A LOT!

Let's take one more detour. My U.S. Naval Academy classmate Rear Admiral Kyle Cozad's life changed in March 2018 when he fell and injured his spinal cord. At the time of his fall he was the Chief of Naval Education and Training. Despite surgery to correct the injury, he lost all feeling below his waist and was told he would be a paraplegic for life. In other words, the response to the question "Will I walk again?" was "NO".

In this interview, Kyle reminds us "don't let anyone tell you what you can't do" as he shares how he moved onward and exceeded his doctor's expectations. Listen to the episode and learn how Read Admiral Cozad set priorities, demonstrated persistence, and recovered.

There are no short cuts. If you are pursuing government contracts, be in it for the long haul and be persistent. When companies look for short cuts and fail to execute a disciplined strategy for engaging the market, it's evident to everyone. This includes government buyers and your teaming partners. If you don't help yourself, others catch on and won't make the effort to help you.

Stand out. Follow this advice and propel your company _onward_ in GovCon.

To listen to and subscribe to the Onward Podcast, visit:
https://emilyharman.com/onwardpodcast

* * *

Emily Harman has 38 years of service to her country as both a Naval Officer and civilian, retiring as a member of the Senior Executive Service in May 2019. A trailblazer, Emily was in the sixth class of women to graduate from the U. S. Naval Academy. Commissioned a Supply Corps Officer, Emily was one of the first two officers on the U.S.S, Emory S. Land, AS-39 to qualify as a Supply Corps Surface Warfare Officer. Recognized as a role model, Emily served as a Company Officer and Leadership Instructor at the Naval Academy.

As a Department of the Navy (DON) civilian, Emily served as a Contracting Officer for professional services and major weapons systems in support of Naval Aviation. Her last assignment was Director of the Department of the Navy's Office of Small Business Programs where she served as the chief advisor to the Secretary of the Navy on all small business matters.

Upon retirement, Emily founded the Onward Movement which seeks to inspire at least 10,000 people to embrace authenticity and release the fear of judgment so they can pursue their dreams with confidence. She guides her clients on a path to lead an authentic and fulfilling life through her Onward Accelerator Coaching Program. Emily also hosts the Onward Podcast featuring authentic conversations on facing adversity and moving forward.

Emily received a B.S. in Physical Science from the U.S. Naval Academy and a M.S. in Acquisition and Contract Management from the Florida Institute of Technology.

Connect with Emily on LinkedIn:
https://www.linkedin.com/in/emily-harman-cpcm-8580413/

MARKET ENTRY AND DIFFERENTIATION

Chapter 4.
Case Study in Multiple Revenue Stream Diversity in Government Contracting

By Eric "Doc" Wright, PhD

Founder, Vets2PM

According to the Small Business Administration, or SBA, over half of the U.S.'s 30 million companies are "microbusinesses", defined as 1-9 employees.[1] Microbusiness go by other official labels too, like SO/HO for small office/home office, or solopreneurs, because over 50% of them have only one employee working out of their home, i.e. the kitchen or the garage.[2] Generating sales, i.e. revenue, and turning it into cash to keep these small companies, hereafter referred to as micros, alive and growing beyond themselves, can be a real challenge.

One way to grow additional revenue streams or diversify your revenue streams is to add the federal government customer. That's because they are the world's largest customer, spending $4.8 trillion, yes, trillion, last year in 2020, and, by law, they have to pay on time. The Federal Acquisition Requirements (FAR), i.e. the law, says they have to![3]

However, this takes work! And if you don't have a dedicated infrastructure, teams, resources, money, and chops, it will take a lot of work! And massive amounts of hustle. That's what this book is for though!

---

[1] https://www.investopedia.com/terms/s/smallandmidsizeenterprises.asp
[2] http://bit.ly/homebasedbusinessandgovernmentregulation
[3] https://www.acquisition.gov/far/52.232-25

It, along with Amazon's *Game Changers for Government Contractors*, *Insider's Guide to Winning Government Contracts*, and access to the Federal Access Platform managed by RSM Federal, you'll have the tools, templates, techniques, and instructional videos to help you build these capabilities. *I know because I did it.* In 90 days! I share that journey in this chapter.

First, I'll share the impetus for my government contracting, i.e. GovCon, journey. It is quite a twisty-winding ride with lots of elevation drops! You'll need a seat belt! Second, I'll explain the basic X's and O's you have to check off to run the fundamental plays necessary to get into the GovCon game. My intent is to save you a bit of time, money, effort, and heartache by sharing with you what I have learned creating the battle scars I have thus far.

The reason for my journey was simple. It was the result of an unprecedented civil and economic lockdown resulting from COVID-19 and the resulting loss of multiple funding sources for my company and non-profit's products and services that followed and are still rippling across our economy. My company, Vets2PM, makes a living recruiting and inspiring transitioning service members and veterans with post-service professional careers in the civilian workforce, or what I call the civilian division (CIVDIV); training them for those target professions with experience translation and credential training; preparing them with 2-page executive resumes, interview skill's development workshops, and LinkedIn usage workshops, and providing them with lifetime placement and mentorship services.

To date, in just five years, we have helped 860+ veterans achieve meaningful, lucrative post-service careers in project management, cybersecurity, building safety, and human resources at over 620 companies, including Fortune 500 like USAA, Microsoft, Boeing, and Booze Allen Hamilton, nationally recognized non-profits like Wounded Warrior Project, and federal agencies like Defense, Homeland Security, and Interior. Our veteran alumni are collectively managing $6 billion in project portfolios, making an average starting annual salary of $95,000.00 USD, which creates $80 million in economic activity in their households, communities, employers and their own businesses, and our great Nation's economy.

However, even though we are a virtual company delivering training worldwide via the Internet, we had a sizeable live training division, delivering our products and services globally throughout the Department of Defense (DoD) global footprint of forts, posts, camps, stations, and bases.

It vaporized overnight with the President of the United States' travel ban. In fact, the night President Trump banned international travel, I was only hours away from boarding a plane to Ramstein Airbase, Germany to deliver a Keynote to base senior leadership and dignitaries and a weeklong training bootcamp to key personnel throughout multiple units at the airbase. "Thank you for your decisive action on international travel, Sir"! I would have been quarantining in Atlanta, Georgia's Hartsfield-Jackson International Airport for 14 days upon my return! Ugh!

And that was only the first domino to fall, the catalyst for the ensuing massive chain reaction of falling dominoes. We had multiple additional funding sources dry up as well. You see, not only do we train, we place. Hiring froze immediately! Corporate America had to first painfully figure out how to right size both its staff and its capital assets portfolios before growing staffs and footprints! And how to Zoom! Or when and where to wear what types of masks. The list goes on and on and is growing daily.

Regardless, 70% of our booked revenue was gone almost overnight. We had to adapt. Quickly. Or die. And my promise to keep my employees employed and paid so their families stay fed is one of the most solemn promises I meet each day. I do not take it lightly. Our lives literally depend on paychecks, which depend on revenue, cost discipline, profit creation, and keeping cash on hand. My folks eat before I do. Literally. We rallied from Mike Tyson's infamous punch in the mouth philosophy. Multiple times!

Over the next several months, from April to September, we would:

1) Enter the civilian project manager (PM) professional development market;

2) Stand up Vets2PM Publishing and release our first book;

3) Develop and successfully beta test 4 "digital MIL2CIV career pipelines", or DCPs;

4) Become an authorized training partner with the Project Management Institute (PMI), US Army COOL TA, and the Institute of Professional Certified Managers;

5) Reorganize ourselves as an "educational institution" to better serve government program-funded veterans in our pipelines;

6) Form 7 industry relationships to expand our catalog of products and services to increase our market cap;

7) Certify our entire staff with Scrum Alliance's Certified Scrum Master to enhance individual and collective new project/program commissioning, execution, and funding;

8) Provide on-demand self-service to corporate America's internal talent acquisition and external recruiting professionals with PurpleX subscriptions, saving them money and time;

9) Streamline and SEO our Website for ease of use and increased on-demand self-service options;

10) Stand up an office in Florida with full video, photography, marketing, and training room capabilities to support other local small businesses in Brevard County;

11) Be featured on Montel Williams' Military Makeover;

12) Contribute to several books helping veteran businesses, small businesses, and government contractors (GovCon) grow their businesses; and

13) Stand up a government contracting ("GovCon") division, serving both federal agency customers and those contractors doing business with the government, i.e. business-to-government sales (B2G).

In 90 days!

Please note, although we help veterans enter new, meaningful, lucrative post-service careers, we are not a Veteran Service Organization, nor a non-profit (although I started a 501(c)3 too!). We are a Limited Liability Company; we live and die by the value of the products and services we bring to market. And we like it that way! Our veteran clients and corporate America customers vote for us time and again to help them solve their problems, with their dollars. That means that what we do must be valuable to them, or they'd quit purchasing our products and services!

Additionally, in the civilian workforce, many times, you are expected to fund your own professional development before you get to training camp to play for that company in the business arena. This means we don't do "free"; we do lowest-cost most-valuable. And we're transparent about it. No ambiguity on our part in the market to confuse unsuspecting or uninformed consumers. Just proven results. Supplying high-quality, high-impact products, services, and staffs.

So, to create as many income streams as possible and to diversify our income stream portfolio, our first adaptation was the idea to enter the civilian project manager (PM) professional development market. It came to us through inquiry and discovery. We noticed an uptick in calls and emails from our veteran PMP alumni across corporate America inquiring about how to earn Project Management Institute-required professional development units (PDUs) to maintain their certifications; especially during the COVID-19 lockdown! We realized many of the traditional PDU-generating methods were being hindered, if not outright precluded because of the lockdown.

We also realized that "achieving meaningful, lucrative careers" is not just the purview of veterans re-entering the workforce after their service. Civilians want that too! So, these two factors led us to create the PDU University (www.pduuniversity.com), a digital catalog of on-demand courses that busy professionals can take to help them preserve the time, money, and effort they spent earning their credentials by keeping those credentials current through continuous learning. My crew tirelessly produced over 60 hours of PMI-approved instruction in just 5 weeks! Thank you, Team!

The second intra-COVID-19 adaptation we made was to stand up the already-cash-flow-positive-in-only-its-first-quarter revenue stream Vets2PM Publishing, to publish the Amazon Best Selling *101 Lessons Learned from Helping Military Members and Veterans Achieve Meaningful, Lucrative Post-Service Careers*. In fact, due to the overwhelming support of this book through sales, testimonials, and interest by veteran authors wanting to contribute, we will be releasing a new edition each year! As of this writing, we already have 29 veteran authors lined up for next year's second edition! Additionally, we are currently working on an additional five more titles, all to be released in 2021! Whoa! Get ready to Amazon the business and inspirational sections of your bookshelf with us! You'll love it!

Our third adaptation was to develop and successfully beta test 4 "digital MIL2CIV Career Pipelines", or DCPs. I can't share our secret sauce with you on how we do this, but I can share with you that in addition to our wildly successful Vets2PM pipeline, we have successfully implemented a DCP for transitioning service members and veterans into cybersecurity, human resources, building safety as code enforcement officials, and big data. Results are early, and COVID-19 still has DOD travel locked down, but they are already promising! And veterans are already achieving meaningful, lucrative post-service careers in these new fields, our only mission!

Our fourth adaptation was to expand the number of organizations that recognize us formally as training partners, which means they promote us to their customers and clients organically. This increases our reach and industry standing while keeping marketing costs low for us. Additionally, it, along with strong, consistent flow of elated customer testimonials have allowed us to generate a word-of-mouth advertising rate of 48%! We are "Authorized Training Partners" with PMI, the US Army COOL TA program, and the 501(c)3 Institute of Certified Professional Managers housed within James Madison University's College of Business.

The fifth COVID-19 adaptation we made to diversify our income streams was to reorganize ourselves as a formal "educational institution" to better serve government program-funded veterans in our pipelines. The Florida Department of Education's Commission for Independent Education has approved us for recommendation to the Florida Veterans Affairs State approving agency, who then approved us for recommendation to the federal Veterans Affairs. As of this writing, we are still awaiting final federal VA approval, but communications from them indicates a favorable review.

The sixth adaptation we made to diversify our portfolio of income streams was to form 7 new relationships with complementary training and GovCon teaming partners. In fact, we secured a formal SBA All Small Mentor-Protégé Program to better serve the Departments of Defense and Labor.

AgileDad, LurnAgile, VA Vet Tec-approved provider Applied Technology Academy, and the Cyber Bytes Foundation allows us to expand our catalog of products and services to increase our market cap to tens of millions instead of ones of millions. This allows us to serve more transitioning service members and veterans. In fact, we now cover about

35% of them with viable, meaningful, and lucrative post-service career opportunities.

Another adaptation we made was to invest in our staff. Due to the nature and magnitude of the environmental and market black swan events, we needed to ensure we could stay adaptive. And lean. And efficient. We did so by codifying our loose agile thinking and infrastructure by training and certifying all of our staff in Scrum Alliance's Certified Scrum Master (CSM) certificate. This allowed us to crystalize an extremely beneficial Scrumban-type organization, which has been able to help us maintain our above-industry-averages financial performance, even under these volatile times! Wow!

The eighth adaptation we made was to convert our internal, proprietary talent database of cleared, credentialed, experienced, and talented veteran professionals to a subscription-based model. This provides corporate America access to our PurpleX database in an affordable, on-demand, self-service style so corporate America's internal talent acquisition and external recruiting professionals can do their job just as effectively as pre-COVID-19, but with more cost and time efficiencies.

Another adaptation we made, the ninth one, was to streamline and SEO our Website structure and content to maximize comprehension, responsiveness, user self-service, and user experience (UX). This has translated directly into increased visitors and dwell times, sales, and followers. It also allows us to add additional Digital Career Pipeline's easily and effectively, i.e. additional vetted, viable business opportunities we choose to pursue.

Our tenth adaptation to increase and diversify our revenue stream mix was to acquire and build-out a physical office in Brevard County, Florida. This office houses a full IoT-driven suite including a conference room, coffee bar and lobby, podcast studio, YouTube video studio, a training room complete with individual cloud-based laptops, and a full post video and audio production area to create logos, brands, commercials, and Websites.

Small businesses on Florida's Space Coast can now create their small business brands and share it with their markets to grow their revenue, or have a professional staff do it for them! (Thanks, JDot Media!) A half dozen investors are already courting us to franchise! Incidentally, we needed the training room, and office to house records, at a physical address in Florida, for the DOE and SAA. We purchased it, and so much more! It's already an asset; not a liability!

Another adaptation was on-boarding our marketing efforts internally again, using the team to cover down. This strategy, along with leveraging personnel relationships and our growing network of industry and professional organization partners, helped us really target our messaging, and resulted in a television spot! We have been featured with PMI on Montel Williams' Military Makeover special (Thanks Montel! Go Navy! and thank you PMI!).

Another result of our combined marketing internalization and consolidation (and publishing adaptations) facilitated a twelfth adaptation opportunity; contributing multiple chapters to multiple Amazon best selling books. We stay in our area of expertise to ensure our readers receive maximum value. Our readers are small, small veteran, and small government contractors (GovCon) because we can help them grow their businesses with proven techniques and tactics to increase receipts, productivity, and profitability.

Finally, our thirteenth adaptation to diversify and grow our revenue streams was adding a revenue stream for the federal government. In fact, it's this adaptation that landed me a ticket to participate in this book! (Thanks Michael!) This decision was the combination of multiple other factors.

The first of which is that I am the leader of the organization. I couldn't help but feel like I wasn't doing enough for my team; for the life blood of the company; or for the economy in which we operate. We had to diversify our revenue streams. Enter GovCon!

Second, during my tenure as a civil servant, I worked in Vendor Pay, paying federal contractors. I worked as a Contracting Officer's Representative (COR) and government receiving official and I was a senior project and program manager. I was responsible for purchasing project-supporting products and services from government contractors. This means I understand the FAR, DFAR, and the government arena. Therefore, I can help the acquisition teams we support, i.e. the Small Business Officer, Contracting Officer, COR, the federal functional, project, or program management customer, and the prime and/or sub-prime federal contractor/contractors serving them.

Third, because of my company's status as a Service-Disabled Veteran-Owned Small Business (SDVOSB), coupled with my expertise as a COR, I was selected to be a member of Solvability's GovCon Master Mind Group that puts on a national annual GovCon Summit. I am a member because I specialize in supporting those GovCon's that are Veteran-Owned Small Businesses (VOB) or SDVOSB. In fact, at each year's conference, Vets2PM sponsors the VOB/SDVOSB Track to educate, mentor, and network veteran attendees. This relationship has also allowed me to add a sub-GovCon revenue stream as an independent Certified Coach with RSM Federal.

As you can see, GovCon streams can be large, stable, and guaranteed post-award. This means that if you add one to your revenue stream mix, you can realize more profitability, which can increase your survivability and longevity. With that case made, I'll now show you how to set up the essential fundamentals. The other authors in front of me and behind me in this book can help you with the intermediate and advanced fundamentals. They're GovCon Experts!

Setting Up Your Essential Fundamentals

So, first things first. You will need to file your business with the secretary of your state. This allows you to open a business bank account. Then you pick your industry classification codes, called North American Industry Classification Codes.[4] These tell the government customer which products and services you offer in which niches. This is followed by securing a DUNS Number[5] and then registering your company in the federal System for Award Management (SAM)[6] to obtain a cage code[7] and the beta.SAM systems to find federal customers with opportunities you can bid on.[8]

---

[4] https://www.naics.com/search/
[5] https://www.dnb.com/duns-number.html
[6] https://sam.gov/SAM/
[7] https://www.fsd.gov/fsd-gov/answer.do?sysparm_number=kb0011119
[8] https://beta.sam.gov/

I also signed up for a monthly subscription to the tools, templates, videos, and email support I get through RSM Federal's Federal Access Platform[9] and certified coach network.

On my own, in less than 90 days, I was able to independently set up a separate Website page specifically for government, a must do, a government business card with all of the above information on it, another must do, a capabilities statement, a must do, and develop my value proposition. Essentially, I demonstrate to potential government customers how we are just the same as everyone else, except we also specialize in X! Or Y! Or Z! That candor and capability create connection, trust, and opportunities.

How do I know what X, Y, and Z are though? Easy! I asked! I have had phone or email conversations with contracting and small business officers about future opportunities and more importantly, current problems they're having! I have also had conversations with people in my network that work in the agencies I serve. I know firsthand what their problems are. This yields opportunities to offer solutions, that they then go contract for. My team has learned that we can win because we understand their problems! I also helped our government prospects write the solution to fix it! It's their idea! To use my products, services, or staff!

One final point before I close. Accruing past performance and helping the government meet its needs and carrying active contracts with government customers on your books can also make you a much more attractive target for acquisition, if you desire. All business owners will exit their business at some point in the future. All. You might as well make it on the terms most favorable to you!

So, speaking of closing and of the future, I hope that you have found this chapter encouraging, practical, and helpful. I deeply appreciate you reading it. The time you voluntarily spent out of your life is precious. I want to ensure the trade was worth it for you!

---

[9] https://federal-access.com

Remember, be proactive to reduce the impact of negative future black swan events, and to exploit the rare opportunities created by positive ones. Diversification is a strategy proven successful in many other areas and disciplines in life. Therefore, I would encourage you to consider adding a GovCon revenue stream to your revenue mix, to leverage diversity in your revenue streams portfolio as well.

The benefits are many. However, the work required is much. But the community shares. And helps. A rising tide lifts all acquisition team member boats! Prepare now so you can proactively position versus reactively responding after an event! Consider a coach too! Even if only through email support. It can save you hundreds of wasted hours, increased levels of frustration, and thousands of dollars in fees and frivolous activities.

Carpe diem!

* * *

Eric "Doc" Wright, PhD, is a decorated military veteran, serial founder of Vets2PM, LLC and VPMMA 501(c)3, business philosopher and linguist, and 3x Amazon best selling author. He authored the book _How To Speak Civilian Fluently: And Prove It!_ to teach veterans and the civilian labor force the language of _management_ and prove it with their internationally-recognized Certified Manager credential from the nonprofit Institute of Certified Professional Managers. His work in _management_ fluency has helped tens of thousands of military veterans, managers, contractors, and government personnel achieve meaningful, lucrative careers and businesses! Vets2PM is the 2019 and 2020 Department of Labor HIRE Vets Gold Award Winner in the small business category for its veteran hiring initiatives!

Secure your small business coaching with Doc at:
https://federal-access.com/ericdocwright/,

Find him on LinkedIn as _docwright2012_ and at:
www.vets2pm.com/blog.

Chapter 5.
GOVCON Economics of the PMP© or Sec+

By Eric "Doc" Wright, PhD

Founder, Vets2PM

Introduction

You can't be anywhere near government contracting (GovCon) for more than about ten minutes before you hear some version of the maxim "this business is all about the relationships!" That's because business, any business, *is* all about relationships, and relationships are all about trust. "Can I trust this person to do what they say they'll do, to the standards they agreed to, in a timely manner, so I make good on my obligations to others that trust me?" In GovCon, this is especially true.

For two reasons; first, the importance of trust-based relationships is especially acute in the GovCon arena because professional reputations, accountability to taxpayers, and national health, defense, and well-being are all on the line to some degree or another. This includes almost every single acquisition! Second, this premium on trust in relationships is even larger in GovCon because the entire construct of the Federal acquisition system rests on small teams of responsible, accountable, capable individuals. Maintaining reputations, decreasing risk to reputations and capability, and delivering as promised is paramount for every member of what the Federal Acquisition Regulation (FAR) labels the *acquisition team*.

The FAR states that the acquisition team "begins with the customer and ends with the contractor providing the product or service".[10] So, regarding this definition, with respect to developing opportunities in GovCon, we can identify several key team members. First, we have the government's representatives: the contracting officer (CO/KO), the contracting officer's representative (COR), and potentially either a regional Small Business Administration (SBA) Procurement Center Representative or an Office of Small Disadvantaged Business Utilization (OSDBU) Representative, hereafter referred to Small Business Officers (SBO). Second, we have the government end-user, the Program and/or Project Manager (PM). Last, we have industry, the Contractor (CTR) and its Contract Manager (CM). As you can see, to deliver full value to the government, and ultimately the taxpayers, the acquisition team has a mission that puts a lot of stock in trust-grounded relationships to deliver. Professionally, timely, and accurately.

How do you increase that relationship's stock price in the government's mind though?

Essentially, first you have to meet them. Second, you must get to know their wants, needs, challenges, and responsibilities. Third, you have to confidently, clearly, and concretely demonstrate that you are capable of delivering what you agree to, literally, so they can make agreements with you. Capability is the keystone in GovCon relationships.

In the solicitation process, you will demonstrate your capability to be in trust-based acquisition team relationships through your management resume, "Section M" of the Solicitation Bid Package, via the "Evaluation Criteria", or both, which you'll submit in your Solicitation Bid Package. You want the government to see you as technically capable, technologically innovative, and heavy on business acumen, responsibility, and accountability. This sense of wide, deep professionalism can increase your stock price, which lessens the risk to form and maintain a beneficial relationship with you. This results in more opportunities to win, perform, and close contracts successfully with the other members of the acquisition team, to grow revenue.

One way to validate the capabilities you communicate is by possessing the right certifications. In the GovCon space, the Project Management

---

[10] https://blogs.managementconcepts.com/working-as-an-acquisition-team/

Institute's (PMI) Project Management Professional (PMP©) and CompTIA's Security+ (Sec+) go a long way! That's because most of the work provided to the government is project-type work. A large share of that project work is in IT or cybersecurity and if it's a US Department of Defense (DoD) opportunity, it's highly likely you'll need access to a DOD IT system at some point in the project lifecycle. This can mean that in a sizeable portion of the opportunities you pursue, these aren't nice-to-have credentials, but must-have credentials...required by policy, regulation, or statute! If you don't have them, you won't be competitive or even be considered for the opportunities.

Project Management Chops

Proven project management know-how is not only in high demand commercially, but also within the government. The fact is that whatever portion of government work is not administering the organization, is project work! This means that GovCon is heavily project based! Therefore, project management knowledge, skills, and abilities are necessary. Having project management chops increases the chance of you performing the contracted work successfully. This capability increases your stock price significantly among acquisition team members because they can trust you to deliver. You have the know-how and you have proven it!

You can increase your stock price even further by validating your project management experience and capability with an independent third-party stamp. PMI's PMP© is considered the gold standard in project management credentials. In fact, for many opportunities, it may be required that at least one member of the contractor's team hold a PMP certification! Today, many Federal requests-for-proposals (RFP) now specifically require that the winning contractor program and/or project managers be certified PMP.[11] For example, Office of Management and Budget (OMB) Circular A-11 states project management certifications are "[…] required for program and project managers in the Federal Government that are assigned to major acquisitions."[12] Additionally, the Project Management Improvement and Accountability Act (PMIAA) recommends a formal federal project and

---

[11] http://bit.ly/GovConRequiringPMPCert
[12] http://bit.ly/FACPPMvsPMPLetter

program management career field with associated credentialing, meaning a growing number of agencies are recognizing the PMP and PgMP (Program Management Professional) as the primary project management credentials.

And it's not just the federal government either. For example, the state of Florida requires its Department of Management Services Public Procurement Professionals to hold a PMP.[13] That's because the statute states that for contract values "[…] in excess of $10 million in any fiscal year, at least one of the negotiators must hold a PMP from PMI."

Additionally, a PMP can also increase the stock price of other acquisition team members too. In fact, National Contract Management Association ("NMCA") Fellow and AT&T Government Solutions' Senior Contracts Manager Jean Marceau, as well as Brendan Johnson, SBA's Head of the Contracting Activity said, "[…] today's contracting officers and contract managers are encouraged to prepare for tomorrow by achieving dual certification in a technology field or in the project/program management fields. This is because the profession returns to its roots in being a trusted business advisor for program success." As with the PMIAA, they go on to mention the Project Management Institute (PMI) by name in a list of major credential players. In fact, I obtained my PMP while serving as a COR for a DoD component.

Cybersecurity Chops

In the DoD environment especially, CompTIA's Sec+ is the must-have certificate.[14] You are certified in the basics of computer, information, and IT system security, and thus able to access DoD IT systems. In fact, it is mandated by a DoD compliance policy; DoD-Directive 8140/8570.[15] DoD 8140 updates the 2006 8570 requirements. The policy states that the Sec+ "is required for all government employees, military service members, contractors, or others who have approved clearances to DoD networks to perform information security roles".

---

[13] http://bit.ly/PMPProfessional
[14] http://bit.ly/RequiredCertsForSecPros
[15] http://bit.ly/WhyTheCompTIAExam

GOVCON Economics of the PMP© or Sec+

The economics of possessing a PMP or Sec+ as a member of the acquisition team, regardless of which role on that team you hold, are clear. They may be required and they can advance the KO's, COR's, SBO's, and PGM's business acumen and careers. Holding the credentials checks-off some professional development blocks. Plus, studies show that PMP holders often receive a pay premium for having it; on average of about 22%.[16] Additionally, *government contractors* and their contract managers can be more competitive, on a higher volume of bids, if they hold the PMP and Sec+. This means that there are opportunities available only to adequately credentialed contractor management teams; which means less bid competition on these opportunities. It also means that every single one of your competitors' teams that don't have at least one PMP holder, or teams that are not Sec+ certified if they are operating in the DOD space, can't even bid! These factors combine to mean more awards for you, and more awards for you means more revenue for your company! So, regardless of where you sit on the acquisitions team, the positive economics of holding the PMP and/or Sec+ are clear. It is in your favor if you are a credentialed holder!

Contractor Recommendations

As we conclude this chapter, I wanted to leave you with a couple tactical recommendations that you can implement fairly quickly. Each one also has a couple associated tips too. These can increase your expertise and capability in the eyes of the government's acquisition team. Remember, capability is the foundation for the trust-based relationships with the acquisition team.

The **first set of recommendations** I have concern your company's website, your capabilities statement, and your LinkedIn profile. First, ensure your company's website has a discrete Government landing page. It should contain your technical, i.e. quantitative and qualitative stories, i.e. your company's CAGE Code, DUNS #, NAICS codes, along with who you are, what you do, how, for whom, and what past performance value was realized by which customer Agencies. I really like seeing direct, inclusive

---

[16] http://bit.ly/HowMuchDoesAPMMake

"we" language here. You want to create the feeling of being an acquisition team member right from the start.

Second, provide the same material as above, but in a condensed executive summary-type format, on your Capabilities Statement, and your management resume. You want your message consistent and clear across all of marketing materials, saying "I'm capable of delivering value to you! In fact, I have a history of doing so!" A valuable concept to help you keep your marketing clear and concise comes from Donald Miller's ground-breaking book *Building a Story Brand* (2017).

When evaluating "is my message clear, compelling, and actionable?" try this trick! Your brain burns calories when you think. The harder you think about something, in order to try and understand it, the more calories your brain burns. Therefore, when people think about you or your company and whether you can bring them value or not, they burn calories in making a decision. Your message literally puts their brain on a tread mill! As a result, easy messages produce 'workouts' of 1-3; complex messages produce workouts of 7-10. People buy at 3 or less. Have someone who doesn't know you or your company read your materials. Do they get it? If so, it's a 3 or less. If not, make it a 3 or less. Deliver every message you can at 3 or less!

Third, I would tell the comprehensive version of your story in your LinkedIn profile too. In the first person though. Again, you want the reader to feel as if you're on a team with them and that you are having a conversation as they read your story. You want them to feel as though they are getting to know you as they read your profile. Also, big deal here, make sure your profile has a professional, close-up picture of you. You don't want to have shades on because you want the viewer to see your eyes. You want your sparkling eyes wrinkled by your cheeks because your smile is so big and warm! Smile with your cheeks! Give your best Duchenne smile![17] You want to be someone they want on the team! Happy! Positive! Capable!

The **second recommendation** is to have at least one member on your contractor team certify as a PMP© and Sec+. I also recommend that a team member achieve PMI's Program Management Professional ("PgMP©)

---

[17] https://www.healthline.com/health/types-of-smiles#duchenne

because a majority of people in and around GovCon use program and project manager interchangeably. Most of the time when we say "project manager" we are talking about the more senior, commonly recognized program manager, the acquisition team's end-user. Therefore, it just raises your stock price even more if you or one of your team members holds it. It's the senior certificate, so to speak. Achieving PMP and Sec+ meets both award and professional development requirements.

However, it should be mentioned that Non-federal employees can't take required Federal Acquisition Institute (FAI) project management credentials training or receive FAI project management credentials (such as the Federal Acquisition Certification for Program and Project Managers (FAC-P/PM). However, the government does want acquisition team members certified in project management, regardless of whether they are government or industry. So, FAI signed a Letter of Understanding with PMI, allowing them to accept the PMP as a comparable substitute for the FAC-P/PM. Therefore, your PMP carries recognized weight with the government!

Meeting the requirements means you're competitive on a larger volume of bids; ones that your competitors can't compete with you on. Which means more awards... which means more revenue! Now you can invest in your staff's professional development and compete on even more opportunities! Lather, rinse, repeat to growth!

Conclusion

Regardless of which role you have on the federal acquisitions team, PMP and Sec+ certificate holders make competitive, competent, capable federal acquisition team members. These credentials can enhance your career and increase your salary. They can help you generate more revenue for your company because you're competitive on a larger volume of bid opportunities. So, whether you are government or industry, achieving your PMP and Sec+ are easy and cost-effective ways to enhance your professional capability. Train your government staffs. Train your industry teams. The GovCon economics are clear, you will benefit in a number of ways!

* * *

Eric "Doc" Wright, PhD, is a decorated military veteran, serial founder of Vets2PM, LLC and VPMMA 501(c)3, business philosopher and linguist, and 3x Amazon best selling author. He authored the book *How To Speak Civilian Fluently: And Prove It!* to teach veterans and the civilian labor force the language of *management* and prove it with their internationally-recognized Certified Manager credential from the nonprofit Institute of Certified Professional Managers. His work in *management* fluency has helped tens of thousands of military veterans, managers, contractors, and government personnel achieve meaningful, lucrative careers and businesses! Vets2PM is the 2019 and 2020 Department of Labor HIRE Vets Gold Award Winner in the small business category for its veteran hiring initiatives!

Secure your small business coaching with Doc at:
https://federal-access.com/ericdocwright/,

Find him on LinkedIn as *docwright2012* and at:
www.vets2pm.com/blog.

Chapter 6.
Mastering the Game of GovCon

By Jenny Clark

CEO, Solvability

Are you an Unstoppable Entrepreneur?

An Unstoppable Entrepreneur does not give up when someone asks them "how do you monetize that?"

Somewhere between the idea, the proof of concept, the willingness to work for free, and risk all you can is the bridge that can be federal contracting. Our nation needs defense innovators to take up the call to start companies and grow them into a sustainable defense ecosystem.

We all know that the defense acquisition system is slow, and in many places broken. Rules that were set up years ago and incorporated into the Federal Acquisition Regulation (FAR) also keep our most Unstoppable Entrepreneurs from mastering the game of GovCon. For a startup business to make it in federal contracting, they have to fund themselves and use whatever free resources are available including the Small Business Administration (SBA) and the Procurement Technical Assistance Centers (PTAC) to get started. It is taking them months just to get registered in the System for Award Management (SAM) and *they are getting scammed by people that charge for that free service*. Next, they turn to their friends and colleagues for help, who are willing to help to some extent but cannot commit the time it takes to help them get started. Others want to join their company but need to be paid. It is not enough that they see the value of what is being created, because no one can afford to put their own financial security at risk to join someone else's dream.

Imagine if there was a virtual accelerator network for entrepreneurs in federal contracting, especially for those who hire veterans with clearances. I choose that subset, because these defense entrepreneurs are the most critical to our national security and closest to the support of the warfighter. They hire veterans who have the commitment, the understanding, the resilience, and the determination to make it all work. We need these defense entrepreneurs now more than ever. They cannot do it alone. They cannot keep showing up for pizza and beer at an innovation center and collaboratively solve our nation's toughest challenges without better funding and better infrastructure.

In his book, _The Unstoppables: Tapping Your Entrepreneurial Power,_ author Bill Schley explains how we need millions of startups just to keep up with China, which is using centralized resources to produce and steal information, while we flail about with failing innovation bureaucracies that prevent our best defense entrepreneurs from succeeding where we need them most.

To build the virtual accelerator network, we must overlook borders on the map and within organizational funding objectives. What we are doing through collaboration and the GovConSummit community, with its Match Alliance, Innovation Alliance, Target Alliance, Compliance Alliance, and Human Alliance, is creating a bridge of trust that connects the nodes of the network, including military and federal agencies, state and local economic development groups, entrepreneurial service organizations, thought leaders, subject matter experts, and professionals with the federal contracting companies at all levels that are committed to our national defense.

The objectives of this chapter are:

1) Outline what successful defense entrepreneurs have overcome to create growth in federal contracting; identifying Inc 5000 leaders in government services.

2) Inspire today's defense entrepreneurs to reverse-engineer what worked over the last decade and find a way, within the collaborative network of the GovConSummit community, to

overcome barriers to success and reach their own Inc 5000 status by 2033.

Objective #1: Identifying what Success in Federal Contracting Looks Like

Do you have what it takes to succeed in Federal Contracting?

What does it take to reach the next level?

How far do you want to go?

Where are the companies and success stories that serve as your role models?

In the past, it was difficult to find the top small businesses in federal contracting.

For many years, I have been tracking small businesses in federal contracting from their early stages. They rarely show up on lists and they are hard to find. We all know they are there. You can find them on the SBA Dynamic Small Business Search (DSBS), but that does not show if any of them have done any federal prime or subcontract work. You can try going to SAM.gov and download listings and filtering by location and NAICs codes. You can use USASpending.gov to find small businesses that have won contracts and some will show subcontracting data. The best resource for potential teaming tied to agency awards is one built by my friend Tim Hagerty, called TeamingPro.com.

My network contacts ask me: "how do I get a list of the small businesses in federal contracting outside DC, Maryland, and Virginia (DMV)? How do I find teaming partners in Tampa Bay, Orlando, Jacksonville, Augusta, Charleston, San Antonio, Colorado Springs, San Diego, Norfolk, and Virginia Beach?"

That list of successful and emerging small businesses does not exist for companies outside DMV. I cannot tell you how many times I have run downloads of those lists, sorted and filtered, and just found them too unwieldy to get valid data, especially when some of those companies may not be around in 5 years. We are always starting over, instead of building up the viable businesses.

Checking for state-level data, many states celebrate their defense contracting base by looking at contract awards. Reporting tends to be based on manufacturers and only on prime contracts. How do you find the small businesses in federal contracting that are subcontractors on prime contracts, and the ones that are primarily services? Identifying those companies and fostering more growth is the fastest way to develop high-paying technology jobs. It is also a great way to keep veteran talent in the state after they transition from the service; especially for those who prefer to stay in defense and possess the leadership, training, commitment, cultural fit, and clearances.

There is no easy way to pick the winners, no easy way to find and follow them to see who stays in the game! We are missing out on the potential of these companies when they do not have the resources, relationships, and revenue they need to grow. This means we are missing out on economic growth and job creation for our defense communities.

The Washington Technology Fast 50 is a ranking system for small businesses in federal contracting. The Fast 50 compares companies that apply and submit financial information and ranks them on their first year Compound Annual Growth Rate (CAGR). There are so many smaller businesses having success in federal contracting, creating economic growth and building communities, that are completely ignored by economic development groups. To me, there is no better business model in the world than one that imports federal dollars into the local community and creates jobs and wealth.

The Inc 5000 list focuses on America's fastest growing private companies. From the Inc.com website, the combined power of the Inc 5000 list for 2020 had a median growth rate of 165% and generated $209.7 Billion in total revenue with nearly 600K jobs added.

On the 2020 Inc 5000 list, there were 242 companies listed under Government Services. There may be other federal contractors listed under their primary industry as Engineering Services, IT Systems Development, Security, Manufacturing, and other specialties. For these 242 companies, the median growth was 174% with total revenue of $15.1 Billion, adding over 20K in jobs.

Like many of you, my entire career has been in the defense industry. I've watched the growth and impact of the defense industry on communities since the 1980's.

Recently, I had a theory that we could look at the INC 5000, for Huntsville, Alabama (home to Redstone Arsenal, NASA, Missile Defense Agency, and other units) and we could show what it takes to grow as small businesses in federal contracting. Uniquely, the Huntsville/Madison County community created the institutions for success back in WWII with Operation Paperclip, which brought Werner von Braun and his team of rocket scientists to the United States, initially to Fort Bliss, TX and White Sands, New Mexico.

Huntsville abounds with the stories of these Peenemunde Pioneers who moved to Huntsville to work at Redstone Arsenal and live on Monte Sano Mountain starting in 1950. Until that time, Huntsville's only claim to fame was as the watercress capital of the world.

In reviewing the Inc 5000 list to find the success stories in federal contracting, I chose to analyze the Huntsville metro area, anchored by NASA Marshall Space Flight Center, Redstone Arsenal, and the Missile Defense Agency. Madison County, the City of Huntsville, the Huntsville/Madison County Chamber, the University of Alabama Procurement Technical Assistance Center (PTAC), the Catalyst Center for Business and Entrepreneurship, and Huntsville Area Small Businesses in Advanced Technology (HASBAT) are among the leadership groups supporting small business growth in federal contracting.

It comes as no surprise to see 23 federal contractors on the Inc 5000 listed in the Huntsville metropolitan area. [18]

Huntsville Inc 5000 List	
Rank	Company Name

---

[18] inc.com/inc5000/2020

981	Aleta Technologies
1139	Cintel
1423	Crossflow Technologies
1890	Linc Research
1896	Hill Technical Solutions
1986	R2C
2338	EngeniusMicro
2344	Cortina Solutions
2347	Simulation Technologies
2417	Integration Innovation (i3)
2426	Martin Federal
2483	nou Systems
2580	Summit 7 Systems
2766	IronMountain Solutions
3382	Noetic Strategies
3464	Trideum Corporation
3536	Sentar
3898	Bevilacqua Research Corporation
4221	Mission Driven Research
4313	Torch Technologies
4397	Monte Sano Research Corporation
4464	nLogic
4501	CFD Research Corporation

What does this list tell us about small businesses in federal contracting? Of the 31 companies listed for Huntsville, 23 of them are federal contractors. Using TeamingPro.com, I was able to find their SAM.gov record and their USAspending.gov data which I used to validate these companies as federal contractors with their contract amounts.

Combined, this group has cumulative prime contract awards of over $4.3 billion and cumulative subcontract awards of over $2 billion, all under three primary NAICs codes: 541330, 541512 and 541715. Based on their SAM.gov registration date, the oldest company registered in 2002 and the youngest registered in 2013. The average number of years for the companies, based on registration date, was 13 years. Most had been on the INC 2000 list in previous years.

What is their impact on jobs, veteran hiring, economic growth, the tax base, and the ability of the region to grow? I will leave that question to the experts at the Huntsville/Madison County Chamber of Commerce.

Why is this important to you as a small business in federal contracting?

It shows you that it takes 7 to 10 years to get traction and acceleration in federal contracting. For me, it validates the Solvability GovCon Small Business Growth Model that I developed in 2018 and is at the core of the Annual GovCon Summit.

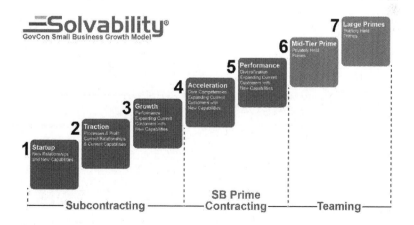

What Huntsville's INC 5000 profiles can tell you is how long it can take and how fast you can grow, provided you have the community support systems required, economic development groups, and a professional workforce that understands federal contracting and federal agency commitment to small business. Together, these, state, and local resources come together to protect and grow the industry.

In developing your own strategy for growth, studying the success stories in Huntsville may be easier than trying to find the same information in the D.C., Maryland, and Virginia regions.

The companies that understand the GovCon Small Business Growth Model and take it to heart recognize that they want to do everything they can to accelerate their business growth. The odds are stacked against small businesses in federal contracting today…unless they have a strong team of mentors and advocates, subject matter experts, and business coaches in an economic development area committed to federal contracting.

What started as an annual conference supporting small businesses in Tampa Bay in 2016, has evolved into an annual GovCon conference called the GovConSummit. Adding a weekly 'FreedomFriday' group call during COVID shutdowns has turned it into a national virtual community and accelerator dedicated to small business growth in federal contracting.

The theme for GovConSummit 2021 of Mastering the Game of GovCon, spotlights veteran entrepreneurs in DoD contracting who hire veterans with clearances and their unique challenges; such as Cybersecurity Maturity Model Certification (CMMC), human capital management, and new business development and capture strategies to grow their revenue in the ongoing and post-COVID environment.

Objective #2 Guidance for the Defense Entrepreneur to Overcome Obstacles

In our community for entrepreneurs in federal contracting, we recommend the following:

Starting day one and every month of operation, here are the questions to ask yourself:

- Where am I?

- Where do I want to go?
- What do I need to do today to move forward?

Creating revenue is the number one objective of any business. Without customers, you have no purpose and nothing to manage. In federal contracting, your number one focus is on your pipeline and your forecasts, improving the methods, accuracy, and control as you build your team and your company.

You decide constantly:

- What customers should we go after based on their 2 to 4-year forecasts?
- How do we move opportunities through our pipeline?
- What actions do we start now that will be important to our success in the next 2 fiscal years?

You will ask the same those questions every month. Every month you will adjust for what has changed and what actions you can take. So much of what happens in federal contracting is outside your control, including:

- Decisions over how the agency plans to award the work
- Access to the work based on contract vehicle
- Strategies of your competitors
- Selections of set-asides that exclude your company
- Delays in funding and decisions
- Protests

What can you control?

- The kind of work to go after and a method for identifying, qualifying, and filtering opportunities
- The resources you have and how you deploy them in business development and capture
- Your pricing strategy and how you manage your costs to meet your goals for growth

Mastering the Game of GovCon means understanding what is required to succeed and gathering those resources, relationships, and revenue to make it all happen. Just like in any other business, perform a SWOT analysis measuring your Strengths, Weaknesses, Opportunities, and Threats. Focus on areas critical to your success:

- Relationships
- Capabilities
- Contract Vehicles
- Past Performance
- Key Criteria

Relationships

GovCon is a **relationship** game, where you find others who will team with you, so the entire team has strengths, without revealing your strategy to competitors or sharing too much with teammates. This is so much like the game of **Clue** where the goal is to determine the mystery of Mr. Boddy's death: who was the killer, with what weapon, and what room? In GovCon, you have "frenemies" and "competitmates." These are companies that you may team with to go after a specific opportunity or program, with whom you have developed relationships and trust. That does not mean that either you or they will not be on opposite sides on other projects.

Capabilities

GovCon is also a game based on **capabilities**, just like any other sport or competition. To get the attention of the customer, you show what problem you solve for them. You cannot just show up and say: "We do Information Technology" and ask: "Do you have any problems that you need us to solve?" That would be like playing the game **Battleship** and asking the small business representative or contracting officer if you got a hit on D-4! As Joshua Frank explains in _An Insider's Guide to Winning Government Contracts,_ you should communicate "Your Value in 45 Seconds!" showing the value you bring, proof of what you have provided, and how you are different from the competition.

Contract Vehicles

Just like any serious competitor, you challenge yourself, improving your game to move up and compete at higher levels. You find the agency customer and know there is a problem you can solve for them. The question is: how does that agency or DoD customer get to you? This is a question of having **Contract Vehicles** or access.

How do you do it?

First, you get subcontracts with major prime contractors on existing programs for that agency. Next, you get on teams that serve that agency as a group, going after major contracts and programs. You search constantly for opportunities to win prime contracts with purchase orders, Simplified Acquisitions, definitive contracts, or Blanket Purchase Agreements (BPA) from that agency's forecasts and postings.

Your next step may be going after **Contract Vehicles**, e.g. GSA Schedules, getting on IDIQs (Indefinite Delivery Indefinite Quantity), or GWACs (Government Wide Agency Contracts). Just like in the game **Monopoly**, you find ways to generate Revenue. In Monopoly, you buy that green Pennsylvania Avenue when you land on it, mortgaging something if you have to, knowing that when you have all three greens, including North Carolina and Pacific, that you'll own the street! What properties or Contract Vehicles do you need to own to generate revenue in your core areas? How much will you have to spend to get on those vehicles? *Will the revenue you win be enough to pay for the costs of going after those contracts plus pay down your line of credit* (mortgages in Monopoly)?

Past Performance

In GovCon, the process to win contracts includes proving that you can do the work. Prime contractors and federal agencies considering your company want assurance that you have the experience to perform the work in addition to reducing their risks. Over time, your company ratings show up in CPARs (Contractor Performance Assessment and Reporting System), which is used by contracting officers and others to evaluate and rank contractors.

Past performance includes contracts your company has successfully executed with commercial or federal customers, as a prime or subcontractor, and work performed at state and local levels. Over time, you build-up skills that enable you to bid on more complex work, with higher risks and more unique requirements. Past performance is like the game of **Life**, where you build on your life experiences until you finally accumulate enough to succeed and win. Just like in the game Life, your choices from the very beginning and along the way determine whether you'll end up in a posh penthouse with a pile of cash… or in a tiny rental apartment working for someone else for the rest of your life.

Key Criteria

More and more contracts come out with requirements that have been crafted by competitors. *Crafted by Default* means that a capture team was able to get some unique requirements listed in the statement of work or elsewhere in the proposal requirements so that fewer companies can meet them. Crafted by default means that the proposal requirements were cut and pasted from another proposal or contract and ended up on the list, whether they are important to the current work or not.

Over time, your company will develop key criteria or differentiators that are unique. Building on core competencies and developing differentiators for your customer story are important to your success in GovCon. Much like the game of **Risk**, you have to understand what your competitors have that you lack, while simultaneously using your agility, daring, and strategy to win.

Conclusion

Mastering the Game of GovCon takes an understanding of the federal market, as well as patience and resilience. To me, federal contracting is an overlooked growth engine that more defense communities should encourage and invest in due to the long-term impact of our small businesses in the defense base and the valuable jobs it creates, especially for our number one defense asset: Veterans.

Are you ready to be a part of this defense entrepreneur movement? I invite you to join me and my colleagues, at whatever level you choose. Connect with me on LinkedIn, join our GovConSummit community group on LinkedIn, participate in our weekly FreedomFriday sessions with GovCon leaders, participate in our Annual GovConSummit, or become a part of our annual membership programs within the GovConSummit community.

Or just pass the word to others you think would be interested. We all share a role in our national defense, an obligation to our nation's Veterans, and the commitment to take action in our local communities, protecting ourselves and our families.

* * *

With over 35 years working in the defense industry, Jenny Clark shows Veteran entrepreneurs how to find financial freedom in federal contracting.

When veteran entrepreneurs succeed, they hire more veterans, supporting families and creating strong communities. She cares about Veterans and their families from her own family's legacy of military service and a desire to create a community where Veterans and their families can finally unpack and settle in.

Since founding Solvability in 1997, Jenny has helped thousands of small businesses with the financial systems and strategies they need for exponential growth in federal contracting. Called the "Oprah" of Federal Contracting, Jenny celebrates the top small businesses in federal contracting each year, based on her benchmarking of the professional services organizations listed on the INC 5000 list. She hosts the awards ceremony at the Annual GovCon Summit, which brings subject matter experts and industry insiders together with small business leaders for networking and education.

The best way to connect with Jenny is through LinkedIn:
https://www.linkedin.com/in/solvabilityjwc/

Join the GovConSummit community and join-in on her weekly online discussion group, FreedomFriday from 1300 to 1330 eastern every Friday.
https://solvability.com/freedomfriday/

To accelerate your business in federal contracting today with Jenny's business coaching, apply using the link below:
https://solvability.com/iammitch/

Chapter 7.
Branding Yourself as a GovCon SME

By Michael LeJeune

Partner at RSM Federal, Podcast Host – Game Changers for Government Contractors

A few years ago I was at a training session with James Malinchak. James was one of the first millionaire's on ABC's Secret Millionaire and to my knowledge, the only person in my field that's ever been on the show. During one of the breaks, I asked James what his most important lesson was from the training. He didn't blink. He said, "Mike, you need to understand right now that somebodies get paid more than nobodies. If you can get this concept deep in your bones and then do what it takes to become a somebody, you will increase your income exponentially for the rest of your life."

Every market has "somebodies" or "leaders" that are undeniably top-of-mind when you think about the products and/or services that they provide. One of your jobs as a business owner is to become one of those top-of-mind companies that people think of when they want YOUR products or services. So how do you become top-of-mind?

Becoming the go-to-choice in your industry involves three key pieces.
1) Focusing on a niche

2) Getting past performance

3) Purposefully branding yourself and your company as the expert

Picking Your Niche

The majority of this chapter is going to focus on item number three on the previous list (branding yourself and your company as the expert), but I'd be remiss if I didn't at least touch on the other two items.

Why is it important to pick a niche? Because you don't want to come across as a jack-of-all-trades company. I sit-in on about 15 to 20 GovCon consults each month. Before I hop on a consult, I always review the website for that company. It never fails that only about 1 out of 20 have what could be considered a niche. And I can't tell you how often I come across a company that does everything from janitorial services to cybersecurity and everything in between.

So how do you brand yourself or your company if you do everything from janitorial to cybersecurity? In my experience, you don't. The messaging is a mess. It's extremely difficult to target an ideal client. Don't even get me started on the difficulty of setting up searches in beta.SAM for all of this. It's a nightmare.

So how do you pick a niche? That's actually an easy question when it comes to government contracting. Do your research. Take a look at the products/services you CAN provide, grab your NAICS codes and keywords, and pull up a few searches in beta.SAM (I talk about this process more in the Building Your Pipeline chapter).

When you are doing this research, you are simply looking for the best opportunity. Out of all of the areas you COULD focus on, where is the best opportunity? The data will help lead you to an answer. Depending on the number of options you have, you can probably do this research in 3 to 4 hours. Maybe less.

Getting Some Past Performance

Once you have your niche, It's time to win some business. Right now you could be thinking, *"You said you need all three to be top-of-mind. This feels like it should be third on the list. Shouldn't I brand myself as an expert first?"* Becoming THE expert in your field is a process. Part of that process is winning some business. I'm not saying you have to win 100 contracts before you can start this process. In fact, you can get a jump on this by looking at your commercial past performance and mapping it to government opportunities. However, the magic isn't going to happen until you have a few government contracts that you can brag about.

Here's one of the most important things to think about when chasing those first few strategic contracts in your niche. When you are reviewing opportunities, I want you to ask the question: How does this build our brand in our niche? If the answer is that it doesn't, you need to understand that this might just be a tactical (revenue) objective for your company versus a strategic (brand building) objective. It's OK to chase a tactical objective, but it shouldn't distract you from the strategic long-term objective of becoming the expert in your field.

Becoming the Expert

A common question for this step is, "should I brand myself or my company as the expert?" The short answer is YES! And you should do them in parallel. Why is this important? Because at the end of the day, people buy from people. They will buy from YOU before they buy from your company.

The other major argument for branding YOU is that you may wake up one day and decide to sell your business, change your business model, or have some other wild idea for a new business. If you ONLY brand your company, you have to start from scratch on your new venture. Branding YOU during this process allows you to build a fan base of sorts that you carry with you no matter what you do or where you go. Starting over is already hard enough. Don't add unnecessary disadvantages to the process.

One of the first aha moments that you need to have is that *experts share their knowledge*. No one is going to know you are an expert if you keep all of your thoughts to yourself. Think about this for a minute. Experts are often called 'thought-leaders.' How did they become thought-leaders? A key ingredient of that process is knowledge sharing. They told the world that they had thoughts on their subject. Not once. Not twice. Thousands of times.

Sharing Your Knowledge

What's the best way to communicate your thoughts? Is there a specific platform? Does one medium work better than another? Should you choose audio, video, text, images, or a combination of all these options?

First off, the options for sharing your knowledge are pretty limitless. In fact, coming up with a new way to share your thoughts, could be part of what makes you stand out from the crowd. That said, I want to share with you a few that are time-tested in GovCon and not going anywhere.

The Subject Matter Expert (SME) Trifecta

When it comes to creating and sharing your knowledge through content, you can choose a lot of options. But I have found these three to be the most powerful. Why? Because these are three places people search the most for experts and knowledge on any topic in GovCon. These are literally the best fishing holes for anyone that could be looking for your products/services. So feel free to use other options as complimentary to these, but these need to be your first options.

A major benefit to these three options is that they work REALLY well together. You can start with any one of them and then slowly add the other two. These are also great for any skill level. They don't require a lot of investment or fancy tools. These are literally the most cost-effective options for branding yourself and your company.

LinkedIn

When it comes to social media and GovCon, there is a clear winner. LinkedIn is a MUST. This is NOT debatable. Twitter, Facebook, Instagram, etc. are options as well, but they are a distant second to LinkedIn. In fact, even if you are using one of those platforms, you still need to be on LinkedIn. Why? Because decision makers, influencers, and potential teaming partners are on LinkedIn. Take a look at the stats here: https://www.omnicoreagency.com/linkedin-statistics/.

This report says over 90 million LinkedIn users are senior-level decision makers. That number is obviously larger than the government market. But that's not a bad thing. In fact, it allows you to connect with both government and commercial decision makers IN ONE PLACE!

Your LinkedIn strategy doesn't have to be difficult. You can start by creating and/or optimizing your profile. Make sure it highlights the niche you want to pursue. Make sure it talks about your commercial and government past performance. Also make sure you put your CONTACT INFORMATION in your profile.

When it comes to your content strategy for LinkedIn, start small. Post a thought, quote, or something each day. Try to comment on a few people's posts each week. Just get started. Over time, you will want to develop a strategy for sharing more thoughts and linking to your other expert content. Just get started and be active on the platform. People will start to message you regularly. Be sure you are responding to those messages in a timely manner.

A Podcast

Podcasts are very near and dear to me. In fact, you likely know about ME because of my podcast. As I write this in 2020, the Game Changers for Government Contractors podcast has over 100,000 downloads. This podcast is the single greatest content machine that I've ever created. It grows while I sleep. I own the show and programming so I decide what people hear. Because I own the content, I get to advertise within it for free.

The podcast was an instant hit, but not an overnight success. In fact, it took us three years to get it to a point that it was driving a massive portion of our revenue. Today, the podcast touches almost all of our clients. If they don't know about the podcast when they become a client, we tell them about it and they become a listener.

One of the reasons that I love podcasting is because it's so easy. You can start by yourself or with an interview style format. There are other formats, but solo and interview podcasts are probably the most popular. Game Changers has both formats. We started out as an interview style podcast and then I added solo episodes in 2020. This has significantly increased our podcast growth and gives me one-on-one time with our listeners.

Here's what you need to start your own podcast.

- A good niche topic
- A hosting platform such as SoundCloud, Podbean, Spotify, etc.
- A format (as discussed above)
- Recording software (you can start with Audacity for free)
- A little time each week for recording, editing, and posting; and
- A good microphone

A Book

Why a book? Hasn't everything been written? A lot has been written, but we are living in a day and age where people crave and consume information at a mind-blowing rate. I have several friends that read one or two books per week! And while a lot has been written, your stories and perspective are what make your content desirable to others.

Here's the deal. There's one strategy for becoming a New York Times bestselling author and then there's a totally different strategy for strategically using your book to put an exclamation point on your expert status. Our focus here is the latter. You don't make a ton of money on book sales. You make money LEVERAGING the book to influence your market and potential customers.

How do you write a book? The good news is that you likely already have everything you need. All of our books are written in Microsoft Word. Once the book is done, it's gets uploaded to our Amazon KDP account. I should note that if you are doing both a print and eBook version, you may have to upload a special edited version for each of those. At the time of this writing, I heard that Amazon was working to clean up this process, but I didn't see a timeline for a fix. It's not a big deal. Just review Amazon's print and eBook guidelines for more information.

Why do we use Amazon? There are two big reasons. Their print on demand service is outstanding. I've used other companies and had issues with printing quality and shipping. Amazon has a great system that makes delivery to your customers almost flawless. The second reason is the reach. Amazon started out in the book business (you may have forgotten this). They have the largest and best network for book searches. This ensures that potential buyers WILL see your book.

How do you organize your book? There's a lot of options. This book for example is organized a little different than our previous two. I have what I call the rule of three. Your book should generally be three sections. Those sections could be called just about anything, but the concept behind them is:

1) An introduction to the topic of the book

2) Your core content and thoughts

3) Your big ideas and strategies to implement these thoughts

The next part of the rule of three's is that each section should have three sections.

1) a beginning

2) a middle; and

3) an end

This format helps you break down the writing into smaller digestible chunks. The thought of writing a book can be overwhelming and any tricks you can pick up will make it easier.

Another trick I have is word count. I usually have a target word count in mind when I'm writing a book. This allows me to break that down by section, author, topics, etc. Again, it just helps with planning and the actual writing of the book. I usually target a minimum of 55 to 60K words. That's about what this book is. It's a great quick read and the writing isn't overwhelming.

That's the format I use when I'm working on a solo book. For a book like this one where you have multiple authors, I tend to use sections instead of the rule of three's. That said, I still use the word count rule. I'm shooting for a minimum of 55 to 60K words. If I go above that, that's fine too.

Leveraging Your Expert Status

In a previous life, I worked with expert entrepreneurs to help them get published. We worked with celebrity authors like Brian Tracy, Steve Forbes, Dan Kennedy, and Jack Canfield. We leveraged their celebrity status to easily make sales and guarantee best-selling books. Now I do this type of work for my company. To date, I have helped over 100 business owners and experts get published and become bestselling authors.

Why am I telling you this? It's not JUST to brag. Although it is nice to name drop and show off a little. My reason for telling you this is that out of those 100, only about 10 or 15 really leverage their status as a bestselling author. It's not because they can't. It's because they haven't followed the simple advice I'm about to share with you. Please don't be an anecdotal tale. Take my advice and change your brand.

Here are six strategies for leveraging your expert status.

1. **Your Signature Block.** Just below my name, my signature block says: "#1 Bestselling Author – Game Changers for Government Contractors" with a link to the book.

2. **Website.** If you wrote a book, put a photo of it on your website. If you have a podcast, make sure there's an image and link to it on your website. We went a step farther and gave our podcast a blog page on our Federal Access membership site.

3. **Social media descriptions.** Take two minutes and update ALL of your social media descriptions.

4. **Capability Statement.** Yes. I'm not kidding. If you wrote the book on your niche, put that in your description on your Capability Statement, also use a photo of your book cover or podcast graphics.

5. **Corporate Overview.** Again, take two minutes and update this. You likely use a corporate overview in numerous spots. Your website is one. Proposals is another. Get this updated and constantly update this as you add to your expert status.

6. **Teaming Partners.** Trying to impress a potential teaming partner? A simple way to do that is to overnight them a signed copy of your book. If you don't have a book, write one! In the meantime, create a thumb drive of your top 10 podcasts, documents, articles, etc.

Getting PAID Because You Are an Expert

Remember what I said at the beginning of this chapter. Somebodies get paid more than nobodies. I like to use RSM Federal as a great example of that. Several years ago, my business partner Joshua Frank wrote a "book" called *The Government Sales Manual*. If you've ever seen the manual, you know why I put the word book in quotes. The manual is over 450 pages and about an inch thick. It's designed to be a desk reference AND a comprehensive "how to" guide for government contractors.

Josh will always be "the guy who wrote the book on government sales" and believe me when I say... this is on purpose. If you are looking for a speaker, consultant, or coach for government sales you want the best. Who better than "the guy who wrote the book on government sales"? That isn't just a saying with us. It's a fact.

Think about that for a minute. I can't tell you how often people call us and say it was down to two companies, but "you guys wrote the book on government sales" and thus we win the business. When everything else is equal, I will almost always have the advantage over my competition by being an author, host of the wildly popular Game Changers podcast (that's how I describe it in my bio), and the guy they see all the time on LinkedIn.

Our company, our team, are all perceived as the top experts in the market because of how we strategically promote our expertise to the market. You can do this by following what we do. Be the person who wrote the book, has the podcast, and continually communicates on LinkedIn within your market.

* * *

Michael LeJeune is a bestselling author and master coach with RSM Federal. Michael hosts the wildly popular GovCon podcast **Game Changers for Government Contractors**, manages the **Federal Access Platform**, and specializes in helping GovCon business owners brand themselves as Subject Matter Experts in their niche. Michael and his business partner Joshua Frank have helped their GovCon clients win over $2.8 billion in government contracts and more than 30+ billion in IDCs. Over 1,000 Government contractors trust the Federal Access Platform as their primary source for GovCon education, training, coaching, and practical strategies for winning government contracts.

Federal Access Platform for GovCon
Get more than 300 essential documents and templates, 100+ training videos, and industry leading Subject Matter Expertise (SME) to accelerate your government sales. You can start your journey with us today for $29 by visiting https://federal-access.com/govconexpertsbook

SALES AND BUSINESS DEVELOPMENT

Chapter 8.
Bridging Government Sales Strategy with Business Strategy

By Joshua Frank

Managing Partner, RSM Federal

Like everything else in business, you need to think in business terms. That means you need to question what you're taught. Don't believe everything you're told. You need to trust your gut.

You may be thinking, "Well, since I know little to nothing about the government market, my gut isn't going to be of much use." Fair point. But that's why you bought this book! It's the reason I wrote this chapter.

There are dozens of non-profits, funded by the government, as well as thousands of industry coaches, consultants, and advisors. *For the most part, they all teach the same concepts*. You need to register in SAM. You need to identify your NAICS codes. You need to contact small business offices. You need a capability statement. You need a bid-match or contract management system to help you find opportunities...

Whether you get direction from one of the non-profits or a paid consultant, you are likely to receive similar concepts, information, and support. Separating average advice from sage advice is not easy.

Let's level-set. More than half of companies that enter the government market fail to win a contract. Most companies and business professionals buy the same books. They attend the same webinars. They attend the same conferences. The level of education is fairly consistent across all companies.

So why do half of these companies, that all receive the same level of education and training, fail to win? The answer is that *they failed to apply* what they learned. They don't have the necessary tactics and strategies.

Successfully and consistently winning government contracts requires that you *think like a business professional, not a government sales professional*.

Do you trust everything other people tell you? No. So why would it be any different in the government market?

Most "experts" teach how to win government contracts but few teach how to do so from a business perspective or provide the resources, tactics, and strategies you need to win.

My chapters in this book specialize on these tactics and strategies. I specialize in the "application" not simply the "education."

To prove my point on the importance of bridging your government sales strategy with business strategy, several anecdotes.

Taking Your Capability Statement to Meetings

Once you've been in the market for any period of time, you'll know that you need a capability statement. Most companies are told, "You need to take your capability statement everywhere you go. You should give it to all government buyers, small business offices, and your teaming partners.

Yes, the capability statement is an important marketing tool for small businesses. However, the guidance given is often wrong.

First, I highly recommend you not simply give your capability statement to everyone you see. Why? Because it's generic! Every government buyer you talk to or meet with; every potential teaming partner, has very specific objectives and requirements. They have specific challenges or issues that change from week to week and month to month.

Here's an example. You're a technology company that provides five core services: cybersecurity, network engineering, software development, database administration, and call center operations. You have a meeting with one of the program managers at Army Material Command (AMC).

You arrive onsite, introduce yourself, and provide her with your business card and a copy of your capability statement.

Okay, let's think about this for minute.

No problem with giving your business card. However, handing her your capability statement is like screaming, "We're a small business!"

Of course she's going to learn you're a small business. That'll take exactly 60 seconds after you start talking to her. But you don't need to shout that you're a small business. Yes, everyone says take a copy of your capability statement to your meetings. Yes, that's the expectation in the government market.

But does it make smart business sense?

No.

But that's not even the major reason why you don't give your capability statement at a meeting.

During your discussion with the program manager, you learn that her current projects, contracts, and challenges involve database issues. The Commanding General for AMC is getting tired of yelling at the technology folks about not being able to see the combined data between three of his systems due to database and interoperability issues.

So, you just finished a great meeting but the capability statement you gave her mentions nothing about database administration in your corporate overview; database administration is the very last service identified on the page; and absolutely none of the metrics, value, or proof statements discuss databases.

When the program manager looks at your capability statement, it looks like database administration is not one of your core competencies and looks to be a secondary service.

Well... that's not what you wanted.

You did an awesome job talking with her and outlining how great your team is at managing disparate databases, but the one item you left behind, your capability statement, doesn't support or augment your claims.

This is why you don't provide copies of capability statements **until after you've had your meeting**. This has nothing to do with government sales strategy. It has everything to do with business strategy.

So, when the program manager asks, "Do you have a copy of your capability statement?" The answer is, "Yes, I'll fire off a digital copy when I get back to the office."

When you get back to the office, spend five minutes updating your capability statement based on what you learned and highlighting which of your services will take care of their current issues and requirements.

You'll move database administration to the top of your list of services. In the corporate overview, you are going to specialize in database administration. In the section on the value you provide, you're going to mention how your team helped an organization (commercial or federal) integrate the data between *three* databases to increase speed of access by 24% and increased the decision making cycle for various business requirements by another 12%.

Now, when the program manager gets your capability statement, they're going to say, "Yes! This is what we're looking for."

I recommend that the only thing you hand out is your business card. No marketing material. No capability statement.

Always have a copy of your generic capability statement with you, just in case. I recommend you always tailor your capability statement after you've met and identified what they're looking for.

Don't Use Agency Logos?

This is an interesting topic because this is the only recommendation I ever make that goes sort of goes against the government guidance. The question is whether or not you are authorized to use military command and federal agency logos on your website, on your capability statement, or on other marketing collateral.

In the chapter on 12 Challenges, we discussed having six (6) seconds for someone to review your capability statement. No one is going to read your entire capability statement. In six seconds, I will understand what your company does, at a high level. But what I really want to know is if you are mature, capable, and have past performance.

You can't convey that in six seconds...*with words*. No one can read and comprehend that fast (fine, some of you can but you are a freak of nature). This is why you'll often see military and federal agency logos on websites and capability statements. In six seconds you can easily convey your past performance. That immediately conveys a perceived strength and capability.

There are some non-profits, small business offices, consultants, and government buyers who will tell you that "you can't use government logos."

Legally and from a regulatory perspective, *they are correct*. In the federal space, all military commands and federal agencies have Public Affairs Offices (PAO) or other entities that deal with the media and the populace. If you visit any of their websites, you'll find that you're supposed to request permission to use their logos.

No one does.

For the most part, large businesses follow the rule of not using agency logos unless being used as part of a case study for a contract they primed.

95% of small businesses ignore this rule. This is why you'll find past performance graphics with logos on many small business websites and marketing collateral.

In my 30 plus years in the government market, I have only experienced a teaming partner, one time, say, "You can't use logos." So much for that company being a strong partner. You're trying to team with them and focus on helping both companies make money...and all they have to say is, "You know...you're not allowed to use logos."

So, what if you become that one company that gets pushback? Then simply tell the government buyer, small business office, or teaming partner that you'll remove the logos and send an updated capability statement. (*But you're only changing it for them.*)

So why do small businesses knowingly (or unknowingly) go against this regulation?

Because you have six seconds.

Because small businesses need every advantage when positioning with buyers and teaming partners.

Because it has nothing to do with government sales.

It has to do with general business strategy.

Are you going to think like a business professional? Use the logos.

You Don't Have to Answer Every Question in A Sources Sought

I love this one! This is a perfect anecdote on the importance of bridging business strategy with government sales strategy.

Did you know that 90+% of contracting officers will accept your response to a sources sought a *week to four weeks after the suspense date*?

Did you know that you can answer as many questions as you want on a sources sought and *ignore questions that you don't want to answer*?

You'll remember from the chapter on 12 Challenges that we have two phases: pre-acquisition and acquisition. Sources sought fall into pre-acquisition.

Since a sources sought is a pre-acquisition market research tool, it does not fall under the same Federal Acquisition Regulations (FAR) that RFPs and RFQs fall under.

What happens if you fail to respond to all the requirements in a solicitation (RFP or RFQ)? You can be pulled-out of competition for being "non-responsive." Well, it's impossible to be non-responsive in a sources sought.

So answer what you want to answer and if answering a question may negatively impact the perception of your company, don't answer it.

You have much more flexibility in pre-acquisition. There's nothing in the FAR that prohibits the government from accepting your response to a sources-sought after the due date.

How cool is this? When I teach these tactics at conferences, even contracting officers come up to me, smile, and say, "Yea, you're absolutely right!"

We Will Not Take Calls

Have you ever looked at a sources sought, pre-solicitation, RFP, or RFQ and seen the statement, "The government will not accept calls. Everything we are providing is in this announcement."

We all have. I'm often asked, "So what can I do to get more information or collect intelligence on the opportunity?

My answer?

Call them.

You can't get in trouble. The government can't remove you from the competition. There is nothing in the FAR that gives contracting officers legal footing to enforce this. They simply don't want to deal with a bunch of contractor questions.

Think like a business professional. We don't let anything stop us from generating revenue.

There is supposed to be a partnership between the government and the industrial base (contractors). This partnership is supposed to be a two-way street. This is how we protect taxpayer dollars and take care of the Nation. It creates a more informed decision and acquisition process.

Over the last decade, government acquisition professionals have become more difficult to talk to. There is a greater fear of protests; a smaller acquisition workforce; and a general culture that feeds into the separation we see today.

Clearly, if we've moved into the acquisition phase (RFPs and RFQs), then the Federal Acquisition Regulation (FAR) clearly prohibits communications that are not documented and shared with everyone else. But if we're in pre-acquisition (sources sought, draft solicitations, general phone calls, meeting with buyers) you are authorized to communicate more freely with the government.

From a government sales perspective, it's fairly clear cut. The government is not supposed to communicate with you, outside of formal Q&A, once an RFP or RFQ is released.

From a business perspective, you call when you're authorized *and when you're not authorized*. Collecting market and opportunity intelligence is what helps you differentiate from the competition and provides you with a competitive advantage when you bid.

If you want to grow your business, then use smart business strategy, trust your gut, and call them - even when they say not to.

Think like a business professional.

Immediately Get 8(a) Certified

When companies learn that they can get 8(a) certified, most hop onto the SBA's website and immediately initiate the process. This seems smart from a tactical perspective but it's a horrible strategic decision for most.

I never tell companies to rush out and get certified for 8(a) (socially and economically disadvantage) until they understand the market and have some success.

Otherwise, you're likely wasting two or more years of your certification. You only get 9 (nine) years and you cannot certify more than once. (On a side note, as executive editor, just as I was getting ready to load this book on Amazon, assuming the President signs the NDAA, SBA announced an extension for all 8(a) certifications to 10 (ten) years *but only* for companies that certified before September 2020. This was due to COVID.

Back to our regularly scheduled programming -

From a government sales perspective, you're told by everyone to rush out and get certified. *Think like a business professional*. Basic business strategy shows that you'll make much more money if you protect those nine years. Don't start the clock until you're ready to take advantage.

One of my good friends, Neil McDonnell, runs the GovCon Chamber of Commerce. This is one of his core positions for minority and socially disadvantaged businesses: don't run out and get 8(a) certified until you understand the market and you have some experience.

These are just some of the anecdotes for why it's so important to bridge your government sales strategy with general business strategy.

Question what you are told through the optics of business strategy. If it doesn't make sense, question it. If you're not sure, ask someone else.

It's more than simply what is available in the market. It's more than simply getting educated. It's about *applying* what you've learned.

Something to think about.

If you want to learn more of Joshua's tactics and strategies, several recommendations:

- **Coaching** to accelerate your business today in federal contracting contact the RSM Federal team using the link below: https://rsmfederal.com/contact/

- Amazon #1 bestseller *An Insider's Guide to Winning Government Contracts* https://bit.ly/GovConInsidersGuide

- Amazon #1 bestseller *Game Changers for Government Contractors* https://bit.ly/GovConGameChangers

- *The Government Sales Manual* https://bit.ly/GovConSalesManual

- Free *Podcast Game Changers for Government Contractors* where we interview many of the industry's top GovCon experts https://bit.ly/GovConPodcast

---

Federal Access Platform for GovCon

Get more than 300 essential documents and templates, 100+ training videos, and industry leading Subject Matter Expertise (SME) to accelerate your government sales. You can start your journey with us today for $29 by visiting https://federal-access.com/govconexpertsbook

---

* * *

Award-winning business coach, professional speaker, and bestselling author, Mr. Frank is a nationally recognized authority on government sales and business acceleration. With 30 years in the government market, he speaks nationally on federal acquisition and business strategy.

He specializes in the development and implementation of tactics and strategies required to differentiate, position for, and win government contracts. Referred to as the *Professor of Government Sales*, his training sessions, highly educational and thought-provoking, are consistently rated the top sessions at national conferences and events.

He has more than 30 years' experience drawn from military service, small business ownership, executive coaching, strategy development and organization design consulting.

Managing Partner at RSM Federal, Mr. Frank is author of Amazon's blockbuster and #1 bestseller *An Insider's Guide to Winning Government Contracts – Real World Strategies, Lessons, and Recommendations*, the highest selling book on Amazon today.

Mr. Frank was awarded Veteran Business of the Year by the SBA and Industry Small Business Advocate of the Year by SAME. A former military intelligence officer, Masters in Management Information Systems (MIS) and a Master's in Business Administration (MBA). Connect with Mr. Frank on LinkedIn https://www.linkedin.com/in/joshuapfrank

Chapter 9.
Building Your GovCon Pipeline

By Michael LeJeune

Partner at RSM Federal, Podcast Host – Game Changers for Government Contractors

Building and growing a successful business starts with your mindset. How you think determines the actions you take and how you perform those actions. If you think you aren't very good at delivering your services, it will come across in every conversation with your prospects. You can try to fake-it-till-you-make-it, but I promise you, your prospects can see right through that.

Your mindset is one of the few things you can control. You can choose to be happy, sad, excited, depressed, etc. Sure, there are outside forces that can influence your mindset, but ultimately you are in charge of it.

Why is this important to building your GovCon pipeline? RSM Federal has coached thousands of companies and I can definitively tell you that the ones that succeed are the ones that have the best mindset. Nothing deters them from their goals. They don't back down in the face of adversity. And maybe most importantly, they see everything as an opportunity.

I talk more in-depth about mindset in episode 111 / "I've Already Won" (https://federal-access.com/ep-111-ive-already-won/) of the Game Changers podcast. Just understand for the sake of this chapter that a positive mindset is critical to how you approach the market, communicate with your prospects, and ultimately how you view opportunities. Now, let's jump-in and talk about your pipeline.

Your Initial Tactical Focus

If you are just starting out in GovCon, you likely have a very tactical or revenue based mindset to how you approach the market. This is fine to start. Eventually, you will also want to think more strategically, but for now, let's talk about some simple tactical aspects of building your pipeline.

Let's start by talking about your research. Companies can spend thousands of dollars digging into the weeds to try to get every data point possible. I don't recommend this strategy in the beginning. You should be able to knockout the necessary research for your market in two to four hours. You can dig deeper later on as you start to develop your strategic focus.

A lot of people are going to disagree with me here, but I have to say that the beta.sam.gov website is actually pretty good. It's different than its predecessors, FBO and FPDS. I get that. And I get that we as humans hate change. Once you look past the faults and look at the value of the data (looks like mindset is creeping into the discussion here again), you will find that it has what you need.

When we start with a client, we start with some very easy searches in beta.sam.gov. I usually pick two to three keywords and two to three NAICS codes. That's it. This is your proof of concept to see what's out there. By the way, this is also a great exercise to perform even if you have been in the market for years.

Once I have my keywords and NAICS codes, I go to beta.sam.gov and perform my searches for contract opportunities. I'm looking to see if there is even a market for these products/services. Again, this is my proof of concept. If nothing shows up, it could mean I'm not searching with the right keywords or NAICS codes. It could also mean the government doesn't buy what I'm trying to sell *or they buy it a different way*. In any case, I'm going to get some great information from this quick search.

Guess what else I'm going to get from this search? If opportunities show up, I'm going to get some opportunities to review for my pipeline AND (this is the real gem here) the contact information for contracting officers that BUY WHAT I SELL. I don't care if you don't plan on responding to the RFPs that show up or if they don't match your business model 100%. What I care about, at this stage, is putting a name to an organization that buys what I sell. Because guess what, they are going on my short-term tactical prospecting list.

Once I discover that there is a proven market for my services, I'm going to set up my Customer Relationship Management (CRM) system to track this stuff. If you already have one, great. If not, please get one. We don't want anything falling through the cracks. A CRM is a great way to keep tabs on your opportunities.

When it comes to your CRM, you can go as simple as a Microsoft Excel spreadsheet or you can use one of the many online tools. Many of the tools out there have a free level. I've found that most of the companies I work with are just fine with the free version of their CRM.

I'm sure your next question is going to be about what tool you should use. I was an early adopter of SalesForce.com. I fell out of love with it over the years as they continued to pile on features. It's still a great tool, but for me, it's overkill. My favorite two options on the market are Zoho CRM and HubSpot CRM. Both tools have a free version. Both tools have a ton of great features. I transitioned from Zoho to HubSpot in 2020 because I was looking for something different in my dashboards with the thought of future integration with our websites. Review them all, and make your own choice. Just keep it simple.

How often should you review beta.sam.gov for opportunities? About once a week. That should give you enough time each week to put a few opportunities into your pipeline. Josh talks more about your time management in the chapter on *A Daily Battle Rhythm* for Government Contractors.

Time to Get Strategic

Now that you are consistently adding opportunities to your pipeline, I want you to start thinking a little more strategically about your pipeline activities. We aren't just looking for short-term tactical revenue. We now need to focus on long-term pipeline building. How do you do that?

Long-term pipeline building starts with Requests for Information (RFI) and Sources Sought (SS). This is your chance to influence the RFP. Your job here is to bend the ear of the contracting team so when the RFP comes out, it's wired for YOU instead of the competition. Just remember, you can't influence the acquisition if you don't respond to RFIs, Sources Sought, or engage your targeted agencies and military commands.

A great thing about RFIs and Sources Sought is that they don't follow the same rules as an RFP or RFQ. You aren't required to answer every question. You can add things that aren't requested in the RFI/SS (this is how you influence the acquisition). And you can even turn it in late. Yes, you read that right. You can typically turn in an RFI/SS response up to a month after the due date. I do recommend that you call the contracting officer and give them a heads up that you are turning your response in after the due date. Why do we do this? The first reason is that it's a great reason to pick up the phone and call the contracting officer. The second reason is that it allows you gather more information about the market research AND ask about other opportunities.

Are you starting to see how your mindset changes the way you look at and perform pipeline management? The average person would find an RFI or Sources Sought that was expired and just move on. The GovCon expert sees this and recognizes that there are several layers of potential here and acts on it.

You can't really put an RFI or Sources Sought in your pipeline. Or can you? The RFI itself doesn't have any cash value, but it should lead to an RFP. This means that the RFI or Sources Sought should go in your pipeline so you can track it, to ensure you don't lose site of it or miss the release of the RFP. It doesn't matter if it's going to be a year out. Put in your pipeline and track it!

Teaming Strategy

Now that we are thinking strategically, it's time to start thinking about teaming opportunities. The best way to look for teaming partners is to identify your top three to five agency prospects and then identify the companies that are already doing business with them. This is a shortcut to winning contracts with your top agencies. You can find all the information you need for this, in you guessed it, beta.sam.gov.

110

Once you have this information, it's still a good idea to pick up the phone and talk to some of the contracting officers and small business reps at your top agencies. Introduce yourself and then ask if they can introduce you to some of the other contractors. Only some will do this. Some will flat out refuse. Most will tell you that they can't endorse a specific company. That's OK. You aren't looking for an endorsement. You are looking for a few names and companies to make your research easier.

While you are speaking with the contracting officers and small business reps, ask about upcoming projects. Dig for information. You are going to use this later when you eventually call potential teaming partners. Here's the deal. If you call a potential teaming partner just because they do business with your potential client, they aren't going to take your call. On the off-chance they do take your call, they will likely be polite, promise to think of you the next time they have a requirement, and then never speak to you again.

However, if you call a potential teaming partner about a specific opportunity that you have talked to their customer about, they are going to take your call. If it's an opportunity they couldn't chase without you (because you have a socio-economic status they don't have), they are going to be intrigued and willing to sub to YOU. How cool is that?

Socio-Economic Statuses

I want to be very clear about something when it comes to ANY status. A status is nothing more than a ticket to the dance in most cases. Think about this. If you are competing on an SDVOSB opportunity, guess what status your competition has? You guessed it. They have the same SDVOSB status as you. What does that mean for your status? Very little.

I don't want to take away from the value of a status, but what I do want to do here is shine a light on the reality. Companies are told every day that their status is their golden ticket to being handed millions of dollars in government contracts. That's just not true. Can you leverage your status to grow your business? Absolutely! But this is just one strategic initiative to consider.

When it comes to your status, start thinking strategically. Use your status with RFIs and Sources Sought to influence the final RFP. Use your status to open doors with teaming partners. Use your status in your discussions with contracting officers to create opportunities that fall under the simplified acquisition threshold. Use your status that way and not as a crutch to build your business.

At the end of the day, you are a business that provides value to its customers. You are not a status. Your status is just ONE tool in your toolbox.

Contract Vehicles

Contract vehicles are similar to your status. They are a strategic decision that needs to be thought out because they are just a ticket to the dance. The real work of traditional business development doesn't stop once you are on a vehicle. Some contract vehicles take significant time to get. For example, as I write this, it takes between 12 and 18 months to get a GSA Schedule. That's not how long it takes to file the paperwork. You could complete your packet and get it submitted in less than a month. The long wait is on the contracting officer side.

Now that I've given you the proper warning, let me explain the benefits of vehicles. The big benefit is that it is a ticket to the dance. That ticket gives you an exclusive right to bid on opportunities or task orders. It also gives you an opportunity to talk with contracting officers and other companies on the vehicle. This is a big deal.

Contract vehicles are your friend. Once you are on them, you must leverage them! Don't just talk to the contracting officer about this vehicle. Use that vehicle to talk to them about other opportunities and to get introductions to other agencies. The same goes for your teaming partners OR other primes/subs that are on the same vehicle as you. Call these folks. Network with these folks. Have teaming discussions about other opportunities.

Responding to RFP's

Selling to the government requires a basic understanding of RFPs. I can tell you from personal experience that the first time you review an RFP, it's probably going to be overwhelming. Here are a few tips to help you reduce your stress and better prepare you for your first or next RFP:

- Review the entire RFP before you decide to respond. Make sure you meet all necessary qualifications.

- If you sell products, ensure that your products meet all qualifications, guidelines, etc. (We have seen PPE requirements for testing, manufacturing locations, and other certification guidelines that have kicked people out of the running.) Review this before you decide to submit.

- Make sure you have the past performance necessary to submit a qualified proposal. Your past performance must be at the volume and / or size of what the solicitation is asking for. Saying you have past performance on a $5 million opportunity when your past performance is a $300,000 contract... is no the size or volume. Yes, you have the exact past performance, but it won't give you a competitive advantage. In this situation, find a teaming partner that has the size and volume for the scope of the requirement.

- Once you decide to chase the RFP, map out all of the requirements and create a checklist. This is called a Compliance Matrix to ensure you've identified every requirement. The matrix will also help ensure that you respond to ALL requirements completely.

- Customize your corporate overview for the opportunity.

- Don't skip ANY sections of the RFP. Skipping a section could get your submission rejected.

- Save time for a comprehensive review before you submit.

- Make sure you submit on time. We've all heard horror stories of RFP's that get rejected because they were 20 minutes late.

- After the RFP is awarded, ask for an informal debrief. Do this whether you win or lose. You want to use this information to improve future proposals.

Strategic RFP's

Sometimes you may decide to chase an RFP you can't win because you are trying to position your company for a future opportunity. Sometimes you will chase small contracts just to get a foot in the door with one of your top agencies. Think about this - let's assume for a moment that you know a $10M contract is coming out over the next year and you don't have a relationship with the prospect. What do you do? You look for ways to get a win. Even if it's a small win. You just need to get in and start your relationship with that prospect. Don't make the common mistake of only chasing the big contracts. Develop a relationship so when that big RFP drops, you will be positioned to win it.

When You Lose a Bid

So how do you add an opportunity to your pipeline when you lose a bid? Here's the beauty about the government. If the government buys it once, they will probably buy it again. If it's a product, consumable, or commodity, you likely know the lifecycle of that product and that allows you to target their next purchase on your calendar. Put that in your pipeline to start tracking the opportunity.

If the government is buying a service, they are likely doing this on a multi-year contract with option years. Read that again. They are using OPTION years. What does that mean for you? That means they may exercise those options, but they may recompete. At a minimum, you know they are going to recompete the contract at its end. Put that in your pipeline.

Here's a question for you. If you lose a bid, can you still get some of the work? The short answer is YES! There's nothing to stop you from reaching out to the winning team to offer your support. Will you get some of the work? Maybe. But this is a way to open a door with that company and talk about other opportunities as well. Think differently about how you approach your losses and find a way to turn them into wins.

Final Thoughts on Your Pipeline

I want to leave you with this final thought. A healthy pipeline solves a lot of problems. Make it a habit to put something new in your pipeline every week, *without fail!* Build your pipeline out 24 to 36 months.

Make sure your pipeline has enough in it to meet your goals. We suggest at minimum a 1 to 5 ratio. This means that if you want to secure 1M in contracts, you need at least 5M in your pipeline. If you are bidding mostly on multi-year contracts, you will likely need a 1 to 10 or even a 1 to 20 ratio because you need to factor in the total contract value divided by the amount of contract years. You may also be facing a situation where the contract ramps up and the yearly amounts are not equal. You need to consider all these factors when looking at your pipeline.

A final complexity to your pipeline is the contract lifecycle. A contract goes through many phases. Pre-acquisition, Acquisition, Award, and then Contract Fulfillment. There is NO set timeline for those phases. I've seen contracts linger in each of those phases. There's also the high likelihood of a protest. These are all things that can delay your company from getting paid. This is also a great reason why you need a healthy pipeline. You can't count on the government to fly through the contract lifecycle and start paying you.

Best case scenario, you are often 60-days from getting paid by the government. That's under perfect circumstances. So keep your pipeline growing. Watch your cash flow. Set the proper expectations for yourself and your team. Follow this advice and you will be well on your way to developing a great pipeline and hitting your business goals.

* * *

Michael LeJeune is a bestselling author and master coach with RSM Federal. Michael hosts the wildly popular GovCon podcast **Game Changers for Government Contractors**, manages the **Federal Access Platform**, and specializes in helping GovCon business owners brand themselves as Subject Matter Experts in their niche.

Michael and his business partner Joshua Frank have helped their GovCon clients win over $2.8 billion in government contracts and more than 30+ billion in IDCs. Over 1,000 Government contractors trust the Federal Access Platform as their primary source for GovCon education, training, coaching, and practical strategies for winning government contracts.

Federal Access Platform for GovCon

Get more than 300 essential documents and templates, 100+ training videos, and industry leading Subject Matter Expertise (SME) to accelerate your government sales. You can start your journey with us today for $29 by visiting https://federal-access.com/govconexpertsbook

---

Chapter 10.
Doing Business with the Department of the Navy

By Emily Harman

Founder of The Onward Movement, President of Emily Harman Coaching and Consulting

This chapter covers how to conduct business with the Department of the Navy (DON) which includes both the Navy and the Marine Corps. These tips apply to other Federal agencies as well; however, there will be some agency specific information and procedures that will not apply across the board.

When conducting business with any Federal agency, you need to be sure you are procurement ready and you must do your homework. You probably hear "do your homework" often and in this chapter, you'll find some practical tips for *how* to do your homework.

Become Procurement Ready

First, complete the ten steps to becoming procurement ready on the DON website. These steps include identifying your North American Industry Classification System (NAICS), obtaining a Unique Entity Identifier (UEI), registering in the beta System for Award Management (SAM) website, and obtaining a Commercial and Government Entity (CAGE) Code. All of these steps can be found on the DON Office of Small Business Programs (OSBP) website under the "Doing Business with DON" tab. (https://www.secnav.navy.mil/smallbusiness/pages/doing-business.aspx)

SAM is an electronic gateway of procurement information. It's a search engine for Contracting Officers, Small Business Professionals, government technical personnel, a marketing tool for small firms, and a "link" to procurement opportunities and important information. It's free to federal and state government agencies as well as prime and other contractors seeking small business contractors; subcontractors, and/or partnership opportunities.

Also register your business in the Small Business Administration's (SBA) Dynamic Small Business Search (DSBS) system. When you register your business in SAM, there is an opportunity to fill out a small business profile. The information provided populates DSBS. DSBS is another tool contracting officers use to identify potential small business contractors for upcoming contracting opportunities. Small businesses can also use DSBS to identify other small businesses for teaming and joint ventures. This is generally a self-certifying database. To register go to:
https://web.sba.gov/pro-net/search/dsp_dsbs.cfm.

Pro Tip: The importance of ensuring your company has a *complete* SAM profile cannot be overemphasized. Your company will have a better chance of being visible to government and large business employees conducting market research if you ensure:

- email addresses for your points of contact are current
- websites and any other links in your profile are current
- you use all of the space provided
- your SAM profile contains specific key words likely to be used in searches. For example, many companies will include Information Technology (IT) in their profile but not the specifics on the types of IT products or services the company offers.

Do Your Homework

Once you're procurement ready, you're ready to do your homework regarding doing business with the DON.

Identify Your Target Customer

The DON has ten buying commands with sub activities under each. It's important to note that the DON's contracting functions are *decentralized* and each Navy and Marine Corps major buying activity purchases supplies and services that support its own mission. A Small Business Professional is assigned to each buying activity. The Small Business Professional is your focal point for upcoming procurements and source for information on small business matters at that particular activity.

Under the command tab on the DON OSBP's website (https://www.secnav.navy.mil/smallbusiness/Pages/default.aspx), you can click on each of the 10 buying commands and find the name and contact information for the Small Business Director, the mission of the command, the top 5 Small Business NAICS for the previous fiscal year, the command's vision, values, strategic priorities, a link to small business opportunities, and a link to the command's Small Business Strategy.

The DON OSBP has several useful videos posted on their website under the Outreach section and on their YouTube channel. There is a wealth of information right at your fingertips. Video topics include:

- Improving understanding and interaction between the Head Quarters Marine Corps Installations and Logistics Contracting Enterprise and Defense Industry Partners
- An Interview with Lockheed Martin
- The Future of the U.S. Marine Corps and Where Small Businesses Can Play a Role
- NavalX and Tech Bridges

Pro Tip: Review the command's website prior to contacting the Small Business Professional. Some companies don't do this making it obvious that the company representative has not done their homework. First impressions are important. This could be interpreted as how your company will approach your work if awarded a contract.

Pro Tip: Many small business owners want to introduce their company to the Director of the DON's OSBP. The Director at the DON level is *not* the appropriate point of contact for selling to the DON commands. The best place to start is with the Small Business Professional at the command that is most likely to buy the products or services your company offers.

Review the Long Range Acquisition Forecast

You can identify current and future procurement opportunities using the Long Range Acquisition Forecast (LRAF). A consolidated DON LRAF is on the DON Office of Small Business Programs (OSBP) website and you will find one for each command on the command's website. The LRAF provides insight into the future procurement needs of the DON. You can find projected contractual requirement descriptions, buying commands, small business points of contact, and acquisition strategies (full and open, set aside, etc.).

You can also click on the "Search what the DON Buys" feature on the DON OSBP website. This feature allows public users the ability to research contract awards and provides transparency in DON's support of the warfighter. This tool is based on historical and publicly available procurement data. This useful information provides users a three-year average of prime contract awards by Contracting Office/Major Command, NAICS, and period of performance based on user specified drill-down filters.

Pro Tip: The DON uses several different contract vehicles so once you identify opportunities in the LRAF, it's important to understand how the command plans to contract for those supplies or services. The command could award a brand new contract or they could place a task order under an existing multiple award contract. Don't be afraid to ask the command's Small Business Professional to help.

Pro Tip: When you review the LRAF, look for subcontracting opportunities in addition to prime contracting opportunities. If you identify an opportunity in the LRAF for which you'd like to subcontract, make note of it and start networking with other companies who may compete for the contract. If there is an industry day, make sure you send a representative as it's an ideal opportunity for finding teaming partners.

Research Contract Vehicles

DON buying activities may post requirements on a variety of available contracting vehicles, to include, but not limited to Seaport-e, General Services Administration (GSA), and other government-wide solutions. Many Navy and Marine Corps supplies and services are purchased utilizing Federal Supply Schedule (FSS) contracts and the GSA SmartPay Card (credit card). Contact GSA for information on how to obtain a FSS Contract and why you should accept the GSA SmartPay Card when doing business with the Navy and Marine Corps.

Pro Tip: Because DON contracting activities are decentralized, it's not useful to ask "Does the DON use FSS contract vehicles (GSA Schedules)?" The question should be asked of each buying command. A better question to ask the command Small Business Professional is: "Does YOUR command use FSS contract vehicles and what do they buy through these vehicles?"

Look at Other Sources of Information

You can find numerous resources on the internet that will provide valuable insight as you do your homework. Some of the resources include the U.S. Navy's Business Operations Plan, Fiscal Year Budget Highlights, and strategies the Navy and Marine Corps leadership developed for their organizations. Listening to senior leadership testify at Congressional hearings can also give you insight into the challenges the organizations are facing. Outreach events and conferences are also valuable sources of information.

Each command is unique. For example, industry has formed Small Business Roundtables at several Naval Air Systems Command subordinate activities. These Roundtables offer fantastic opportunities to network and provide feedback to the government on their policies.

Pro Tip: Reach out to other small businesses that have been successful in winning contracts supporting the command you're researching. Once you become experienced, give back and help less experienced small businesses.

Pro Tip: Familiarize yourself with Federal, DOD, and Navy contracting procedures. You should be familiar with the regulations that apply to your company/s socioeconomic status. Be familiar with Federal Acquisition Regulations (FAR), the Defense Federal Acquisition Regulation Supplement (DFARS), and the Navy Marine Corps Acquisition Regulation Supplement (NMCARS). You can also find a Guide to Marketing to the DOD here: http://business.defense.gov/Small-Business/Marketing-to-DoD

Get to Know the Command's Small Business Professional

Once you've done your homework, it's time to reach out to the command's Small Business Professional.

Pro Tip: Don't call them until you've done your homework! Why is this a Pro Tip? Because many companies ignore this advice.

Pro Tip: When you reach out to the Small Business Professional, do not lead with your company's socioeconomic or size status. Federal government employees are much more interested in the capabilities your company offers and how your company can help the organization achieve its mission than your socioeconomic or size status.

Pro Tip: Here's a recommended format for an email or a script for a phone call you can use when reaching out to DON Small Business Professionals. (Note: make changes appropriate for your company's situation.)

> Good afternoon (NAME OF SMALL BUSINESS PROFESSIONAL)
>
> I am reaching out to you today on behalf of (INSERT NAME OF COMPANY) located in XXXX. (INSERT NAME OF COMPANY) has XXX years of experience in (XXX) and (XXX). Our team has done our homework and researched opportunities to support your command. I'd like to schedule a meeting with you to introduce our company and share how we can help you accomplish your mission.
>
> We reviewed your website and your Small Business Strategy. We've also researched your Long Range Acquisition Forecast (LRAF) and SAM to identify opportunities to support (INSERT COMMAND/ORGANIZATION). In reviewing the LRAF, we found five opportunities for which we are best suited to compete.
>
> In addition, we identified several entries in the LRAF marked full and open competition and we'd like to discuss the possibility of setting them aside for competition among Service Disabled Veteran Owned Small Business (SDVOSB). Our company is a Service Disabled Veteran Owned Small Business (SDVOSB) and we can bring your attention to at least one other SDVOSB that can perform this work.

After our review we have some questions and
would like to set up a meeting with you to discuss our
capabilities and our questions. We'd also like to better
understand opportunities for SDVOSBs like ours to
support (INSERT COMMAND NAME). (Note: if you
can list your questions in the email that would enable
the Small Business Professional to research answers
prior to the meeting.)

I appreciate you taking the time to review this
information and look forward to hearing back from you
in regards to scheduling a meeting.

Pro Tip: When you call the command's Small Business Professional, make sure you know to whom you're speaking. If you're speaking to an administrative professional tasked with answering the phone and scheduling meetings, save them and yourself some time and do not tell them all about your company. Leave that for the actual meeting with the Small Business Professional.

Pro Tip: It's important to remember that government employees are humans. They can be stressed, overworked, sometimes inexperienced, and working under immense pressure. Just like you, they have challenges in their personal lives as well. They're doing their best. Please treat them with respect and make their lives easier by doing your homework.

Pro Tip: Do not send one email and include every DON Small Business Professional in the to, cc or bcc line. This shows you haven't done your homework and that you're not targeting the command that buys what your company sells. It also creates extra work for government employees. Your email should be tailored for a specific person with a specific need or opportunity you'd like to discuss.

Pro Tip: Use the subject line of your email to adequately communicate what the email is about. This increases the chances of the email being opened.

Pro Tip: Do not come across as desperate to win a government contract or only focused on your company's size status/certification. Instead address how your company can satisfy a requirement that supports the command's mission.

Pro Tip: Do not go after only large dollar contracts, especially when you don't have a relationship with people in your targeted government organization. There's nothing wrong with starting small and demonstrating your company's capabilities while developing past performance.

Pro Tip: When you meet with Small Business Professionals, ask for points of contact for marketing to the technical customer.

Pre-Solicitation Activity

The DON OSBP and representatives from each of the ten buying commands attend the Navy League's Sea Air Space event and the DON Gold Coast Small Business Procurement event each year. Details on these events can be found on the internet. In addition, the commands and their subordinate activities typically hold their own outreach events. You can learn valuable information by watching the videos on the DON OSBP's YouTube channel as well.

Pro Tip: Attend an outreach activity with a specific goal(s) in mind. Perhaps you have specific people you want to meet or specific questions you want to get answered. Set an intention before you attend the event. And follow up with people you meet afterwards.

Summary

In summary, although the focus of this chapter is on how to conduct business with the DON, these tips apply to other Federal agencies as well. Just remember, some agency specific information and procedures may not apply across the board.

If you are struggling with doing business with the Navy or any other government agency, you can schedule a free coaching call with Emily to learn more about how she can help you. Visit: https://calendly.com/emilyharman/15min

* * *

Emily Harman has 38 years of service to her country as both a Naval Officer and civilian, retiring as a member of the Senior Executive Service in May 2019. A trailblazer, Emily was in the sixth class of women to graduate from the U. S. Naval Academy. Commissioned a Supply Corps Officer,

Emily was one of the first two officers on the U.S.S. Emory S. Land, AS-39 to qualify as a Supply Corps Surface Warfare Officer. Recognized as a role model, Emily served as a Company Officer and Leadership Instructor at the Naval Academy.

As a DON civilian, Emily served as a Contracting Officer for professional services and major weapons systems in support of Naval Aviation. Her last assignment was Director of the Department of the Navy's Office of Small Business Programs where she served as the chief advisor to the Secretary of the Navy on all small business matters.

Upon retirement, Emily founded the Onward Movement which seeks to inspire at least 10,000 people to embrace authenticity and release the fear of judgment so they can pursue their dreams with confidence. She guides her clients on a path to lead an authentic and fulfilling life through her Onward Accelerator Coaching Program. Emily also hosts the Onward Podcast featuring authentic conversations on facing adversity and moving forward.

Emily received a B.S. in Physical Science from the U.S. Naval Academy and a M.S. in Acquisition and Contract Management from the Florida Institute of Technology.

Connect with Emily on LinkedIn:
https://www.linkedin.com/in/emily-harman-cpcm-8580413/

Chapter 11.
A Daily Battle Rhythm for New Government Contractors

By Joshua Frank

Managing Partner, RSM Federal

When it comes to government sales, many companies experience challenges with time-management and setting priorities. I've been asked a thousand times, "How much time should I be spending on government sales?"

My answer starts with "you're either pregnant or you're not."

As part of your education and training, you will better understand which activities are a waste of your time and which will help you win a contract. You'll find these tactics and strategies on the Federal Access Platform. I'll put a link at the end of the chapter.

At a basic level, you need a foundation.

There are two parts: Getting Started and the Daily Rhythm.

Getting Started

When you first decide that you want to win a government contract, you need to perform a propensity search.

Propensity

*The exercise of researching government contract data in order
to identify who buys what you sell, how much they buy, and
how often they buy it.*

I can't tell you how many companies are bidding on everything they can, without a strategy, and without knowing who they should be building relationships with.

Government sales is not so different from commercial sales. Yes, there are clear differences including time for the sales cycle, but the importance of building customer relationships is market agnostic.

When I say to you, "You should have three strategic targets, agencies, or military commands, to properly identify where you need to build relationships," what is your response? You're likely to say, "Sure, that makes sense. I should be calling and having meetings with prospects that have bought more of what I sell than the other agencies in the government."

Even though everyone agrees, many have no idea who buys what you sell, how much, and how often. This waterfalls into many companies not knowing their three strategic targets.

Propensity

Whether you've been pursuing government contracts for years or you're new to the market, stop everything you're doing! If you haven't identified the propensity for your products or services, we need to level-set and capture that information. Where do you go to find this information? beta.SAM's Data Bank. I created a 1.5-hour training video on how do to this. It's on the Federal Access Platform.

What's Your Value?

Once you have propensity, it's time to map your competencies and communicate the value that your products and services provide to your customers. I discussed the importance of communicating value in the chapter on 12 Challenges.

It's not what you sell. It's not your socio-economic status. It's the quantifiable and qualifiable value of your solutions. It's numbers, metrics, and percentages.

Federal Pipeline Calculator

Okay! You've performed propensity and know which three military commands or federal agencies you should be targeting for the next twelve months. You also know the value that your solutions provide; value that differentiates you from your competition and communicates maturity and capability. Now it's time to identify your revenue objective and how many opportunities you need in your pipeline. How many opportunities do you need to prime and / or subcontract?

There's a pipeline calculator in Federal Access (yes, I keep referring to Federal Access but it has hundreds of templates and resources for everything a government contractor needs to enter and accelerate into the market).

Whether you use a pipeline calculator or a notepad, you need to identify the following:

- What is your revenue target for the year?

- What is your win rate? For every ten bids you submit, how many do you win?

- Based on your annual revenue target, your win rate, and the average size per contract, how many opportunities must be in your pipeline over the next 12 months?

- How many opportunities per month, per quarter?

Without these metrics, you're going to find yourself six months down the road saying, "Yea, yea, yea! I know! I need to do more business development. I've just been so busy with other requirements. I'll focus on prospecting next week."

There will always be "good" reasons why you're not winning contracts and generating revenue. I'm sure they are awesome reasons. I'm also sure you won't hit your revenue target if you focus on your reasons instead the numbers you need to hit.

If you don't prospect, if you don't bid, you don't win.

What are your sales metrics?

Setting-Up beta.SAM

The final part to getting started is setting up automated search queries in beta.SAM (and / or whichever bid-matching or contract management system your company uses).

Setting up accurate and strong opportunity searches takes time. Even when I create a search in beta.SAM, it takes a good month to work out the kinks. My initial search will return several hundred opportunities. I'll find that 60% have absolutely nothing to do with what I sell. So, I login, remove a keyword, add another keyword. I might add a Product Service Code (PSC) and remove the North American Industrial Classification System (NAICS) code. There are a dozen possible changes I'll make. It's not hard. But if you don't understand how the system works, ask for help.

Remember that setting up searches in beta.SAM is not a one-and-done. Be patient and continue tailoring. In fact, you might need four, five, or even a dozen saved searches so that you're not wasting time reviewing opportunities that you can't pursue.

Let's review. There are four activities you want to complete before you go into full market engagement:

- propensity research
- competency-mapping to understand and communicate your value
- identifying revenue and pipeline metrics; and
- setting up your searches / queries in beta.SAM

Your Daily Battle Rhythm

Time management and time-blocking is the topic of this section. Let's be honest, very few of us are strong at time management. If you are strong at time management, *you are a freak of nature*. In America today, business is complex and consuming. For many, you're lucky if you accomplish even a fraction of what you planned on completing for the day. If you're one of those freaks of nature, send me a note on LinkedIn and tell me you're one of them.

As a result, one of the most common questions I field is, "What should I be doing?" followed by "how much time should it take?"

As I mentioned earlier, you're either spending quality time on government sales or you're not. This is not a part-time decision. At the same time, it doesn't have to be 40 hours a week. For some, eight hours a week is enough to complete requirements. For others, it might be 20 hours. Everyone is different. But it all comes down to time management.

Below is a common outline that I provide clients. None of them follow it exactly. But it will help you understand how to look at your own time management.

- **Morning Coffee and Pre-Qualification (15 to 45 minutes).** When you first arrive at the office, grab some coffee, and quickly review all the opportunities that were emailed to you overnight. You're not reading the entire solicitation! You're quickly looking at each opportunity to see if you should do a full qualification later. You should be able to perform a pre-qualification review on any opportunity in 60 seconds. When complete, you'll have a small number of opportunities on a pad of paper.

- **Morning - Responding to Sources Sought and Business Development (1 hour).** Once you're done pre-qualifying opportunities, it's time to focus! From the last couple days, you know that you have a source sought to respond to. You also have several calls to teaming partners, perspective teaming partners, and government contracting officers, decision makers, and champions. Yes, you can do this in an hour! After several responses to sources soughts, you'll have a template you can update in ten to thirty minutes. As for calls, you'll probably connect on half of them. The rest you'll leave messages. You'll likely need to add a couple of those calls to tomorrow's schedule.

- **Rest of the morning - Open (2 to 3 hours).** Take a walk outside. Answer emails. Talk to the boss. Work on other requirements.

- **Post Lunch – Full Qualification, Pipeline Management, and Market Intelligence (1-2 hours).** You get back from lunch and you pull-up those five or six opportunities you pre-qualified earlier in the morning. This is when you perform a full

131

qualification, looking at requirements, the statement of work, etc. Of these five or six opportunities, you decide that two are strong. *This is when they go on the pipeline.* Once they're on the pipeline, you likely know if you can prime 100%, need to bring on a subcontractor, or need to join a team. Perhaps you put an opportunity on the pipeline yesterday and you know that you are going to need to join a team? In addition to fully qualifying the morning's opportunities, you're also making calls to perspective teaming partners on the opportunities you added to the pipeline yesterday or earlier in the week. This time period is also when you're searching beta.SAM's Data Bank for contract data and market intelligence. This is also the time period when you create teaming agreements and continue making calls to the government.

- **Rest of Day - (2-3 hours)**. Answer emails. Work on projects. You can also keep working on government business development.

For the first month or two, yes... it's probably going to take you longer than what I've listed above. *This is why you need to learn tactics and strategies.*

The difference between a job and an occupation is life-long-learning. You're not going to be an expert in government sales overnight. But that also doesn't mean you can't win a lucrative contract in six to twelve months.

Looking at your current battle-rhythm, what do you need to change? Where do you need help? Do you need to block-times on your calendar so other employees are not bothering you during these periods?

What do you need help with?

What are your next steps?

Something to think about.

If you want to learn more of Joshua's tactics and strategies, several recommendations:

- **Coaching** to accelerate your business today in federal contracting contact the RSM Federal team using the link below: https://rsmfederal.com/contact/

- Amazon #1 bestseller *An Insider's Guide to Winning Government Contracts* https://bit.ly/GovConInsidersGuide

- Amazon #1 bestseller *Game Changers for Government Contractors* https://bit.ly/GovConGameChangers

- *The Government Sales Manual* https://bit.ly/GovConSalesManual

- Free *Podcast Game Changers for Government Contractors* where we interview many of the industry's top GovCon experts https://bit.ly/GovConPodcast

---

Federal Access Platform for GovCon

Get more than 300 essential documents and templates, 100+ training videos, and industry leading Subject Matter Expertise (SME) to accelerate your government sales. You can start your journey with us today for $29 by visiting https://federal-access.com/govconexpertsbook

---

* * *

Award-winning business coach, professional speaker, and bestselling author, Mr. Frank is a nationally recognized authority on government sales and business acceleration. With 30 years in the government market, he speaks nationally on federal acquisition and business strategy.

He specializes in the development and implementation of tactics and strategies required to differentiate, position for, and win government contracts. Referred to as the *Professor of Government Sales*, his training sessions, highly educational and thought-provoking, are consistently rated the top sessions at national conferences and events.

He has more than 30 years' experience drawn from military service, small business ownership, executive coaching, strategy development and organization design consulting.

Managing Partner at RSM Federal, Mr. Frank is author of Amazon's blockbuster and #1 bestseller *An Insider's Guide to Winning Government Contracts – Real World Strategies, Lessons, and Recommendations*, the highest selling book on Amazon today.

Mr. Frank was awarded Veteran Business of the Year by the SBA and Industry Small Business Advocate of the Year by SAME. A former military intelligence officer, Masters in Management Information Systems (MIS) and a Master's in Business Administration (MBA). Connect with Mr. Frank on LinkedIn https://www.linkedin.com/in/joshuapfrank

BY THE NUMBERS

Chapter 12.
Financial Freedom in Federal Contracting Comes at a PRICE: It's Your Wrap Rate!

By Jenny Clark

CEO, Solvability

Small Businesses in federal contracting face many challenges - and pricing is at the top of the list. If you're not pricing correctly, you're depriving yourself of the financial freedom you deserve!

How Do I Price?

For companies selling Professional Services, also known as "butts in seats," the pricing strategy all revolves around versions of the term Wrap Rate. The questions are:

1. How much do you pay your employees per hour?
2. How much do you bill your customers per hour?
3. How much do you "mark-up" the pay rate to determine the billing rate?
4. How do you make sure that your billing rates cover all your costs?
5. How do you make sure your pricing is competitive?

In the federal market, the terminology around pricing has different names and may include:

- Wrap Rates

- Loaded Labor Rates
- Burdened Rate
- Fully Burdened Rates
- Fully Burdened Rates with Fee
- Billing Rates

Pricing for federal contracting is based on *labor hours* by *labor category* times the *billing rates* set for each labor category. The *billing rate* includes the *direct labor cost* of the employee pay plus percentages for *indirect costs* to cover *fringe benefits, overhead and general & administrative* (G&A) costs, plus *fee or profit*.

Wait a Minute – I Have to Share My Pricing?

In the commercial world, billing rates are computed the same way. The difference in federal contracting is that you may be required to provide the details of your pricing, showing how you determined the pay rate and the indirect rate and fee percentages.

Not all proposals require this detail. It depends on the type of contract, size of contract, whether you are prime or subcontractor, and several other factors. You may not even know what detail is required until you receive the spreadsheets requesting the cost breakout.

It's important that you fully understand the math of pricing, because there are no standard spreadsheets used for pricing. You don't have the option of creativity in federal contract pricing, because you have to follow directions from:

- Instructions in the proposal and from the Contracting Officer or Prime Contractor
- Federal Acquisition Regulation (FAR) guidelines
- Cost Accounting Standards (CAS)
- Guidance from Defense Contract Audit Agency (DCAA).

What Difference Does it Make?

It is actually more important to keep winning the work and increasing your revenue, contract base and backlog, than it is to be profitable on each contract. Yes, you heard me right! From a "bean counter" that usually emphasizes profit: REVENUE GROWTH for a small federal contractor is more important than profitability on individual contracts. The main strategy in the game of GovCon is to keep growing and OUTRUN YOUR OVERHEAD (the topic of the next chapter). Find a way to avoid the roller coaster of wins and losses so you build a sustainable, growing company!

From a business standpoint, it's about getting the volume of work to cover your indirect costs of fringe, overhead and G&A, and it's the same with any business. It just happens to be more complicated in federal contracting because of how much time and money you invest in getting established as a federal contractor, learning how to:

- Find opportunities
- Write and price proposals
- Upgrade your back office systems and procedures
- Create a team that can capture, win, and execute contracts.

Understanding Your Billing Rate Buildup is the Difference Between Winning and Losing

Price too high, you won't win the work.

If you can't bid and win contracts, you can't sustain the company's growth rate. If you can't grow at a steady rate, you're always at risk of not being able to support the costs of business development, capture and proposal management.

Price too low, you won't cover your costs.

It's tempting to bid on Lowest Price Technically Acceptable (LTPA) contracts when there is a possibility of a large contract or creating a strong agency relationship. When it's a race to the bottom on price, your work is not valued and you'll have a difficult time recruiting and retaining qualified personnel.

Think about this from a business perspective. If you were doing the same work in the commercial world, would you keep going after customers who are always telling you:

- You need to drop your price

- Your people don't have the advanced skills we wanted
- Your turnover is too high

Wouldn't this customer take up too much of your time for it to pay off? And wouldn't that keep you from going after the customers worth having?

If you win contracts, but the revenue doesn't cover your costs, you're at risk because you don't have the profits and cash flow for ongoing investment to scale your company.

Federal contracts for professional services require a line of credit tied to your billings to fund your payroll. If there is any slowdown in billing, any payment or collections issues, or a drop in headcount and billings due to a contract ending, what happens?

Any negative blip, not to mention a global pandemic … and you're not sure how you're going to meet payroll. Early on, you probably skipped your own paychecks, but that's no longer enough to bridge the cash flow issues. It's hard enough to find bankers that understand federal contracting or financing companies that can fund your accounts receivable and payroll.

Your Pipeline has to be X times your Revenue Target!

Many small business entrepreneurs share this dilemma: how do I chase more opportunities when I'm working full time on the contracts we've won?

It breaks my heart to get a call from a company executive who needs work NOW. There is no such thing as NOW in the federal contracting world. There is no such thing as "getting lucky!"

On the Game Changers podcast with Michael LeJeune of RSM Federal (Episode 78), Michael explained the Secret to Revenue Growth. If a company has a 20%-win rate and wants $1 Million in new contracts, they need to have $5 Million in qualified opportunities in their Pipeline! That calculation doesn't even consider the period of performance for the contracts, or how this is affected by prime/sub relationships and how each covers the scope and performs the work (workshare). Do the math yourself based on your current pipeline and ask if you're reasonable about a growth rate of 40% this year.

The larger you grow, the more your company pipeline becomes the machine that maintains itself. Without a solid strategy and the team in place to execute it for you, you'll be constantly hitting plateaus and unable to sustain growth. GovCon is no place for dabblers!

Billing Rate Definitions

The difference between the Billing Rate and the Pay Rate is called the Margin. It's also referred to as Burden. The Margin is the amount built into the Billing Rate to cover Indirect Costs and Profit.

Your pricing includes the Labor Hours by Labor Category, the average Direct Labor Pay rate by employee, and the Margin. These variables - Hours, Pay Rates and Burden are the sources for your profit on a contract.

- **HOURS**: If you price based on getting 10,000 hours, you've effectively put in a volume discount. When you end up with only 1,000 hours, you're losing money on every hour worked. This happens all the time: you have a signed teaming agreement and you're on the winning team. The prime promised 5% workshare and you never get enough work under the contract to justify the investment you made in bidding it.

- **PAY RATES**: If your actual pay rates are higher than the pay rates you used for bidding, you'll lose money on the contract.

- **BURDEN**: If your actual Indirect rates for Fringe, Overhead and G&A are higher than the rates you used for your bid, you'll lose money on the contract.

When the average profit percentage in federal contracting is less than 10%, you can't afford to make a math error!

Now for Your Math Homework!

The percentages shown below for Fringe, Overhead, G&A and fee (profit) are just examples. Below are the two most common methods for computing a Billing Rate based on the employee or average pay rates. Both methods are acceptable and typically an agency chooses one method or the other in its pricing spreadsheets.

I call these methods Left Coast Overhead and Right Coast Overhead. Why? For over 20 years, I didn't even realize there were two methods, so don't think you missed this one either!

There are two different formulas, and they will eventually come to the same result, but you may give away your slim profits if you don't understand this.

- **Left Coast Overhead** includes Direct Labor plus the Fringe in the Overhead Base. G&A is applied to Direct Labor, Fringe and Overhead. Fee or Profit is applied on Total Costs.

- **Right Coast Overhead** includes only Direct Labor in the Overhead base. G&A is applied to Direct Labor, Fringe and Overhead. Fee or Profit is applied on Total Costs.

The companies that were using the Left Coast were subcontractors to SAIC which was headquartered in San Diego at the time. I needed to memorize the equations - and be able to determine which method was in use, so I would follow the correct calculation in the spreadsheet.

It's just a convention for me - one that I've used for years. As the mother of identical twins, I always put them in alphabetical order for photos. I kept the hospital bracelets on their ankles longer than I should have, because I couldn't tell them apart in their diapers! I always put Anne on the left and Sarah on the right - which only worked as long as I was the one setting up the picture.

Right Coast Overhead Formula

The Right Coast Overhead Formula is the simpler method. You multiply the Pay Rate times the Fringe Percentage, then the Pay Rate times the Overhead Percentage. The G&A applies to all three components: Direct Labor plus Fringe plus Overhead. Fee applies to all costs: Direct Labor plus Fringe plus Overhead plus G&A.

Here's the calculation for the Right Coast Overhead Method: (((Direct Labor) + (Fringe Rate times Direct Labor) + (Overhead Rate times Direct Labor)) times (1+G&A Rate)) times (1+Fee Percentage) = Billing Rate	RIGHT COAST		
	Direct Labor		$ 50.00
	Fringe	30%	$ 15.00
	Overhead	13%	$ 6.50
	G&A	10%	$ 7.15
	Fee	10%	$ 7.87
	Bill Rate		$ 86.52
	RIGHT COAST: Overhead Base is Direct Labor Only		

LEFT COAST OVERHEAD FORMULA

The Left Coast Overhead Formula takes the Pay Rate times the Fringe Percentage, then the Pay Rate plus the Fringe Percentage times the Overhead Rate. The G&A applies to all three components: Direct Labor plus Fringe plus Overhead. Fee (profit) applies to all costs: Direct Labor plus Fringe plus Overhead plus G&A.

LEFT COAST		
Direct Labor		$ 50.00
Fringe	30%	$ 15.00
Overhead	10%	$ 6.50
G&A	10%	$ 7.15
Fee	10%	$ 7.87
Bill Rate		$ 86.52
LEFT COAST: Overhead Base is		
Direct Labor Plus Fringe		

Here's the calculation for the Left Coast Overhead Method:

(((((Direct Labor) + (Direct Labor times Fringe Rate)) times Overhead Rate)) times (1+G&A Rate))*(1+Fee Percentage) = Billing Rate

Where Do I Put in the Profit?

Sometimes the pricing instructions will tell you to price without the fee, meaning the fee amounts will be computed and negotiated separately. Be watchful for how the columns are marked and whether the resulting billing rates make sense.

When you are proposing for Cost Plus contracts, the fee will show separately. If you do see pricing that doesn't include any profit or fee, ask for clarification about how the fee will be calculated.

When you are submitting pricing for your Prime Contractor, you'll only show the Fully Burdened Rate and you won't show the details of Direct Labor, Fringe, Overhead and G&A. Your indirect rates and profit are proprietary information for your company. Sometimes companies will share this information initially, not realizing that their teammate may become a frenemy or a competimate in the future.

When is a Wrap Rate a Multiplier?

It gets confusing because people use so many of these terms interchangeably. You may walk into a meeting where everyone comes from another organization, and they start talking about Onsite and Offsite rates, and then start talking about Wrap Rates and Multipliers. This happened to me, and it took me several months to figure out all the definitions and the math. Every time you attend a new team's proposal kickoff, update your math definitions and spreadsheets!

- For some people, a Wrap Rate is a Billing Rate, like $86.52 per hour for an Analyst. If your Billing rate is $86.52, and your pay rate is $50, you will have $36.52 per hour to pay for Fringe, Overhead and G&A and profit, which is the same as 73% Margin ($36.53 divided by $50.)

- For others, a Wrap Rate is the number that you multiply times the Pay Rate to get a Billing Rate. I call that a Multiplier, and could range from 1.5 to 2.0 or higher. If your pay rate is $50, and you have a Multiplier of 1.73, then $50 times 1.73 is the Billing Rate of $86.52. Same result - different terms and different methods. The .73 of the 1.73 is the amount that covers your Fringe, Overhead, G&A and Profit.

- Using the examples below, to compute the Multiplier in a spreadsheet, just change the direct labor amount to 1, and the result will be the Multiplier. It's the same whether you are using LEFT COAST or RIGHT COAST.

- Multiplier Math Tricks:
    - Compute a Billing Rate from the Pay Rate: The Pay Rate times the Multiplier is the Billing Rate.
    - Derive the Multiplier: The Billing Rate divided by the Pay Rate is a quick way to calculate the Multiplier.
    - Derive the Pay Rate: The Billing Rate divided by the Multiplier is the Pay Rate.

LEFT COAST			RIGHT COAST		
Direct Labor		1.00	Direct Labor		1.00
Fringe	30%	0.30	Fringe	30%	0.30
Overhead	10%	0.13	Overhead	13%	0.13
G&A	10%	0.14	G&A	10%	0.14
Fee	10%	0.16	Fee	10%	0.16
Multiplier		1.73	Multiplier		1.73
LEFT COAST: Overhead Base is			RIGHT COAST: Overhead Base is		
Direct Labor Plus Fringe			Direct Labor Only		

More Math: Using Multipliers to Derive a Pay Rate from a Billing Rate

Many times you're getting ready to send an offer to a candidate, or a Program Manager is asking what salary range to discuss with potential new hires. How do you quickly determine the appropriate Pay Rate?

Using the examples above for Left Coast Overhead and Right Coast Overhead, you can see that a Pay Rate of $50 per hour for the sample percentages gives a Billing Rate of $86.52.

10 More Tips About Rates

Let me add to your confusion by explaining Onsite and Offsite Rates. These are also used differently by different organizations.

1. Onsite and Offsite Rates refer to whether there is facility cost (like Rent, Utilities, etc.) included in the Billing Rate.

2. Whichever Billing Rate is higher is the rate that includes facility cost, meaning the work is most likely performed at the Company Site.

3. I call them Onsite and Offsite either Company Site (includes your facilities costs) and either Client Site or Customer Site or Government Site, to reduce confusion.

4. If they are only talking about one set of Billing Rates, read the proposal instructions for guidance.

5. When you're a small company, you usually only have one "Overhead" rate, or you may have a home office or no office space.

6. Sometimes you'll get a list that just says "rates" and you think it's the billing rates. Then you find out those were the pay rates. Or, you'll assume that the "rates" are billing rates, but you think they are the rates including facilities costs and it turns out they were rates to work at. If you get this backwards in your bid, you're either going to be overpriced and sure to lose the bid, or underpriced and doomed to lose money for every hour worked.

7. Know your market and the competitive range - both the pay scale and the billing rates. In the commercial market, you'd be able to talk more to the customer and get more information. You'd also get a feel for what the competitive range is. Not so in the federal market.

8. Pricing on large contracts, like Indefinite Delivery Indefinite Quantity (IDIQ), you'll frequently be bidding rates without knowing the location of the work. How do you consider the differences in pay scales, state unemployment tax rates, workers compensation insurance and the challenge of recruiting people in unknown markets?

9. When you are a subcontractor on a prime contract, you may receive direction about the maximum Billing Rates or the Pay Rate ranges.

Or you may receive no direction at all - it depends on the Prime and your relationships.

10. As Joshua Frank of RSM Federal, author of *An Insider's Guide to Winning Government Contracts* would say "something to think about..."

Considering how much of yourself you dedicate to your business, don't you deserve to earn what you're worth? There is a way to do that. The price of financial freedom is your ***wrap rate***!

If you'd like to learn more, you can download examples at the Solvability.com website:

https://solvability.com/wraprate

* * *

With over 35 years working in the defense industry, Jenny Clark shows Veteran entrepreneurs how to find financial freedom in federal contracting.

When veteran entrepreneurs succeed, they hire more veterans, supporting families and creating strong communities. She cares about Veterans and their families from her own family's legacy of military service and a desire to create a community where Veterans and their families can finally unpack and settle in.

Since founding Solvability in 1997, Jenny has helped thousands of small businesses with the financial systems and strategies they need for exponential growth in federal contracting. Called the "Oprah" of Federal Contracting, Jenny celebrates the top small businesses in federal contracting each year, based on her benchmarking of the professional services organizations listed on the INC 5000 list. She hosts the awards ceremony at the Annual GovCon Summit, which brings subject matter experts and industry insiders together with small business leaders for networking and education.

The best way to connect with Jenny is through LinkedIn:
https://www.linkedin.com/in/solvabilityjwc/

Join the GovConSummit community and join-in on her weekly online discussion group, FreedomFriday from 1300 to 1330 eastern every Friday. https://solvability.com/freedomfriday/

To accelerate your business in federal contracting today with Jenny's business coaching, apply using the link below: https://solvability.com/iammitch/

Chapter 13.
Outrunning Your Overhead

By Jenny Clark

CEO, Solvability

How do you Outrun your Overhead?

Ever say to yourself "I can either work or sell, but I don't have time to do both!"

Or wish you could hire more people for business development... but you're worried about bringing on another person?

Maybe you're waiting until a new contract starts, and that will be the time when you:

- Hire a new business developer
- Invest in opportunity and pipeline management tools
- Upgrade your payroll, HR or accounting software
- Get someone to take the "billable" work you're doing for customers, so you can spend more time developing new relationships

There's never a perfect time - so how do you get the time and the money to grow your company, so you're not constantly on a roller coaster between contract wins and losses.

What if you had a Rate and Pricing Model (RPM) to use for Revenue and Profit projections, for tracking indirect rates and making sure that you're covering all your costs?

For small businesses in federal contracting, especially those focused on professional services and IT, success depends on steady growth in revenue and headcount, while managing your indirect costs, generically called Overhead. Many small businesses struggle to find the balance between growing their revenue and the investment and spending required to support their new contracts. It seems that the more you grow, the more systems and processes are needed to maintain the business development pipeline and to execute and manage contracts.

In the book *Game Changers for Government Contractors*, I shared the GovCon Small Business Growth Model, where companies are all beyond the Startup Stage. These 2nd stage companies are first gaining Traction, then creating steady Growth, and getting ready for Acceleration.

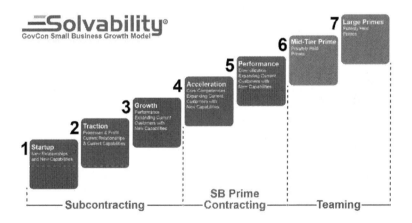

This chapter about "Outrunning Your Overhead" covers basic answers for small businesses providing professional services in the Traction and Growth stage. This is a simple staffing model, where with each new hire the company earns more margin.

What Kind of Financial Reporting and Forecasting Do You Need?

A Rate and Pricing Model (RPM) provides indirect rate estimates, revenue forecasts and profitability tracking.

- What indirect rates should we use for this bid?
- How do we describe our indirect cost pool structure for proposals?
- How do we know if our indirect rates are competitive?
- How do we come in lower on this bid?
- How do we get DCAA to approve our systems?

Let's go through each of these questions and why it matters, so we can make sure your Rate and Pricing Model (RPM) answers these questions.

#1 What Indirect Rates Should We Use for this Bid?

The indirect rates to bid should be in the competitive range for the work that you're going after. When you're under about 10 employees, your actual indirect rates are likely to be higher than the competitive ranges because of how much you'll be investing in business development to get more work coming in.

Your goal should be to figure out what the indirect rates should be in the future, based on where you want to take the company, including what agencies you want to pursue, where the targeted work is located, and how you plan to scale your back office and business development activities.

There are typical ranges for fringe benefits, since to be competitive most companies will match the benefits offered in the market. Fringe costs include payroll taxes, workers' compensation insurance, holiday and other paid absences, and group benefits like health insurance and 401K matching and administration. Fringe benefits range from 10% to 30%, with 10% for payroll taxes, 10% for paid absences and 10% for group benefits.

- Payroll Taxes, Social Security and Medicare total 7.65%, with Federal and State Unemployment and Workers Compensation insurance rounding it out to about 10%.
- To estimate for holiday and paid absences, take the number of days off per year times 8 hours. Usually 80 hours for holidays and 120

hours is a good starting point. Using 10% for leave, with 200 hours of leave allowed in a standard year of 2080 hours.

- Group benefits could be zero percent to 10% or more. The major expenses are group health insurance, and 401K matching and administrative costs. Most employers offer other insurance benefits and Section 125 Cafeteria plans covering Health Savings Accounts, Dependent Care, Flexible Spending Accounts and other options.

General & Administrative Costs are the costs of running the corporation itself. These would be the cost of salaries for Executives, Human Resources, Finance and Accounting plus their associated fringe benefits, facilities expenses and other corporate expenses.

- There are also competitive ranges for General & Administrative or G&A rates, typically 10% to 15% for small businesses pursuing subcontracts that are also under $10 Million in Revenue. Above $10 Million in Revenue, most small businesses find they need to invest in systems and processes to make the company efficient and competitive.

Between Fringe and G&A is the variable called Overhead, which is different for every company. Although Overhead is a term used generically for any indirect costs, Overhead is specifically the support cost of the technical workforce, and depends on the kind of services the company offers its clients.

Overhead includes:

- Expenses for recruiting - recruiting software and advertising, background checks, and other fees.
- Facilities security clearance - cost of verifying security clearances, security compliance.
- Training and certification cost for employees.
- Indirect labor costs and associated fringe benefits for supporting technical workforce.
- Computers, software or equipment used for the technical workforce.

- Facilities allocation for technical employees working in your facilities.

When the technical employees work at a client site or government site, there are no associated facilities costs, and usually the indirect support costs are minimal.

#2 How Do We Describe Our Indirect Cost Pool Structure for Proposals?

In the proposal narrative or the cost volume, you may be asked to describe how you compute your indirect rates. What they are looking for is a description of your pools and how you apply indirect rates. Use the answer to question #1 to write the description of your cost pools (numerator.)

There are several variations, and as your *small business* grows you'll want to consider adding more complexity to your pool structure to suit the type of work you are bidding and the competitive environment. Most companies have at least 3 pools: Fringe, Overhead and G&A. Below are *simplified* formulas for Total Cost Input method:

- Fringe Pool Costs Divided by Productive Labor (where Productive Labor excludes leave and includes Direct Labor, Overhead Labor and G&A Labor)
- Overhead Pool Costs Divided by Direct Labor (Right Coast Overhead Method) or Overhead Divided by Direct Labor plus Fringe on Direct Labor (Left Coast Overhead Method)
- G&A Costs Pool Costs Divided by Direct Labor plus Fringe Applied to Direct Labor Plus Overhead applied plus Non Labor Costs.

If you have significant Materials and/or Subcontracts, you may consider using the Value-Added method, where Materials and Subcontracts and some other direct costs are excluded from the G&A Base (Denominator.)

#3 How Do We Know if Our Indirect Rates Are Competitive?

Competitive indirect rates depend on multiple factors.

- What type of contract are you going after - Cost Reimbursable, Time & Material (also called Firm Fixed Price Level of Effort) or Fixed Price?
- Are you the prime contractor or the subcontractor?
- Are you just trying to establish yourself on a GSA schedule or are you going after a competitive IDIQ (Indefinite Delivery Indefinite Quantity) or an Agency GWAC (Government Wide Acquisition Contract)?
- Are you focused on a niche market with few competitors, or are you going after a broad market where price will be the main differentiator?
- Is the work being bid in markets where there is high demand and competition to recruit and retain employees?
- Is the work to be performed in locations where the cost of living or required taxes and benefits are particularly high?

All of these factors should be considered as you are working on your overall strategy and focus, just like any other business. The difference with federal contracting is that instead of being able to "sell" to your customer, you have to solve their problem, meet their requirements, and give them options on how to buy from you, all with limited interaction in a complex decision-making process.

#4 How Do We Come in Lower on this Bid?

Financial models and forecasts are estimates, and some methods are more reliable than others. In the end, executives prefer to see several alternatives and choose their own winning strategy. Just because last year was a rough year does not mean you need to use last year's rates for bidding. As the company grows and your rates are more stable, you'll probably choose to do that.

What you are looking for is flexibility to show optimistic, pessimistic, and most likely scenarios. As you create the indirect rates to support your proposal, you want the option to decide what set of indirect rates best reflect where you'd be when the contract would start. You're making lots of assumptions about the amount of the award, when it starts and that there will be no delays or protests. So, you may as well set your path for the indirect rates that lead to a win on this bid or don't bother submitting it!

#5 How Do We Get the Defense Contract Audit Agency (DCAA) to Approve Our Accounting System?

There's no way for you to request for DCAA to review or approve your accounting system. DCAA does audits when requested by a Contracting Officer or other federal agency official. A Contracting Officer may request an audit when you are bidding on Cost Reimbursable contracts or when you're about to be awarded a Cost Reimbursable contract. DCAA uses a form called the SF1408 that is available on their website at DCAA.mil. It requires:

- Generally Accepted Accounting Principles (GAAP)
- Clear and separate identification of direct and indirect costs
- Ability to track cumulative costs by contract
- Indirect costs applied consistently
- Under General Ledger Control
- Uses Timesheets to track and identify labor by employee and charge number and tied to payroll
- Update books monthly
- Unallowable costs not charged through to contracts
- Track by contract line items when required
- Production costs don't include pre-production costs
- Tracking of Contract Costs against Contract Value
- Billings can be traced back to details in accounting system
- Accounting data reliable for pricing
- Accounting system operational or planned

Another organization, the Defense Contract Management Agency (DCMA) performs some of the contract compliance and administrative duties as well. You may also have an Administrative Contracting Officer (ACO) responsible for examining your performance. There are times when you'll want to get assistance from DCMA or the ACO on questions about contracting practices.

How Do You Set Up Your Management Reporting as a Federal Contractor?

You have a Pipeline spreadsheet you've been using since the company started. You trust it. It has all your contract data and you update it monthly based on billings so you always know how much your contract backlog is, and exactly when each task order and option year expires.

You've got your Profit and Loss Statements for the last few years, and this year you're determined to create a Budget. You've always been careful about spending. With the contracts you just received you can finally see 18 months out!

What you're looking for is a model that ties your Revenue Forecasts to your current headcount and employees and pulls in last year's actual costs. This model would show you that your costs are covered and that while profit may bounce around every month, the trend shows profit, and cash flow is positive.

Another way to view this is looking at total costs for one year. Make a list of your current employees and their annual salaries. At this point, do not add your anticipated new hires. Add 10% for payroll taxes and worker's compensation insurance. That is your annual labor cost.

Determine your fixed costs for one year, including:

- Rent and Utilities, telephone and internet
- Computer and office expenses
- Marketing expenses and website
- Recruiting software and fees
- Group benefits like health insurance
- Accounting and legal fees
- Interest expenses on credit cards or lines of credit
- Business development costs
- Dues and Memberships
- Travel for customer meetings and business development
- Annual expenses like general liability and workers comp insurance, bonuses
- Property taxes, State and local taxes and licenses

Add your annual labor costs and your annual fixed costs. Divide by 12. That is your monthly baseline operating expense, what it takes to run the company on an accrual (not cash) basis.

Now take last month's billing total - exclude any reimbursable or subcontract costs. Adjust it some and get to a round number that makes sense and that you can carry around in your head at all times. That is your Monthly Baseline Revenue.

Take Monthly Baseline Revenue minus Monthly Baseline Operating Expenses and that is your Monthly Baseline Margin.

This method assumes that you maintain your current headcount and revenue - and it's simple enough to start. Don't get all tied up into adding Revenue for contracts that have not yet started or been awarded. Don't worry about the headcount you'll lose when a contract or task ends.

Your goal here is building a Rate and Pricing Model (RPM) that takes all of this into account and helps keep you on track for your revenue and costs. You're using indirect rates for bidding, so the RPM should also track your actual and forecasted rates for Fringe, Overhead and G&A. With this approach, you'll also meet the requirements to pass the DCAA SF1408 Pre-Award Accounting System Adequacy Checklist!

The goal is to get sustainable revenue, with subcontracts and task orders that start to cover more than six months at a time. Stay on track for no more than 10% of your employees being non-billable and you'll get the traction you're looking for.

Below are some examples from my proprietary Solvability Rate and Pricing Model: The Labor Estimating Model gives a snapshot of the labor costs for your company. It's a starting point for indirect rates forecasting. When you're in Professional Services and or IT, focused on staffing, controlling labor productivity drives your cash flow and profitability.

Labor Estimating Model — copyright Solvability, Inc. 2020

The SUMMARY Income Statement with Indirect Rates provides a top level view of costs and indirect rates.

SUMMARY Income Statement with Indirect Rates	Your Data Entry	Indirect Rate Calculations from Income Statement*								Copyright Solvability Inc. 2020
		Fringe Pool	Fringe Base	FAC Svc Ctr	FAC Base	FAC Alloc	Overhead Pool	Overhead Base	G&A Pool	G&A Base
Contract Revenue	1,564,184									
Direct Costs										
Direct Labor	950,000		950,000					950,000		950,000
Direct NonLabor	10,000									10,000
Total Direct Costs	960,000									
Indirect Costs:										
Fringe	300,000	300,000					292,500		7,500	
FACILITIES COSTS	12,000			12,000						
Overhead Labor	25,000		25,000				25,000			323,000
Overhead NonLabor	4,300				1,200	10%	5,500			
G&A Labor	25,000		25,000						25,000	
G&A NonLabor	136,800				10,800	90%			147,100	
Total Indirect Costs	502,600									
Gross Margin	101,584									
Unallowable Costs										
Interest Expense	2,000									
Other Unallowable Costs	500									
Total Unallowable Costs	2,900									
Net Income	6.76% 99,084									
Total Indirect Pool/Base		300,000	1,000,000	12,000	100%	12,000	323,000	950,000	179,600	1,283,000
Indirect Rates			30.00%					34.00%		14.00%

Overhead Pool includes Fringe on Direct Labor

Total Direct Costs	960,000		G&A Pool	179,600
Total Indirect Costs	502,600		G&A Base	1,283,000
Total Costs	1,462,600		Total Costs	1,462,600

Note 1 - computed using Right Coast Overhead Method   Note 2 - Overhead Pool includes Fringe on Direct Labor

Outrunning your Overhead

Outrunning your overhead means combining your business strategy, your pipeline, your talented team, and your vision, into a model and method that keeps you on track.

As your company grows from the Traction Stage to the Growth Stage, you'll want to stay steady on rates. The Growth Stage is when you'll be going after Prime Contracts and looking at GSA Schedules and other contract vehicles. As you reach the Acceleration Stage, your focus will be on getting more efficient:

- More ruthless about pruning your pipeline
- More investment in infrastructure for systems and processes
- More aggressive in going after long term programs and relationships

Mastering the Game of GovCon never ends!

With over 35 years working in the defense industry, Jenny Clark shows Veteran entrepreneurs how to find financial freedom in federal contracting.

When veteran entrepreneurs succeed, they hire more veterans, supporting families and creating strong communities. She cares about Veterans and their families from her own family's legacy of military service and a desire to create a community where Veterans and their families can finally unpack and settle in.

Since founding Solvability in 1997, Jenny has helped thousands of small businesses with the financial systems and strategies they need for exponential growth in federal contracting. Called the "Oprah" of Federal Contracting, Jenny celebrates the top small businesses in federal contracting each year, based on her benchmarking of the professional services organizations listed on the INC 5000 list. She hosts the awards ceremony at the Annual GovCon Summit, which brings subject matter experts and industry insiders together with small business leaders for networking and education.

The best way to connect with Jenny is through LinkedIn:
https://www.linkedin.com/in/solvabilityjwc/

Join the GovConSummit community and join-in on her weekly online discussion group, FreedomFriday from 1300 to 1330 eastern every Friday.
https://solvability.com/freedomfriday/

To accelerate your business in federal contracting today with Jenny's business coaching, apply using the link below:
https://solvability.com/iammitch/

MANAGING YOUR GOVCON BUSINESS TO SCALE

Chapter 14.
A Framework for Management Mastery

By Russ Barnes

Founder, Systro Solutions

Employees who believe that management is concerned about them as a whole person are more productive, more satisfied, more fulfilled. Satisfied employees mean satisfied customers, which leads to profitability. —Anne Mulcahy

Management is about getting the most out of the people who make up your organization. It's about coordination, cooperation, and communication. It's about the orderly execution of operations on a routine basis. It's about the most effective application of resources. But, make no mistake, it's ultimately about the productivity of people.

People in general are motivated to solve challenging problems and when you limit their creativity, the work becomes a monotonous existence where they do what they have to do...no more, no less. If you want automatons who do only what you tell them to do and who produce only while you watch over their shoulder to make sure they do it the way you want it done, then you should probably stop reading at this point.

I chose not to exist under that type of leadership or to be that type of leader. I desired to be as productive as I could possibly be and I believed that others desired to be as productive as they could possibly be. Knowledge is power. I wanted people to know why their role was important and how to contribute to the mission so they would be more confident and willing to take on greater challenges. I believed that they would succeed in finding the right solutions more frequently and learn

165

more, faster. They would engage with colleagues more constructively, be less anxious, less guarded, less fearful, and more willing to ask questions. To make this happen, during my early days as a leader, I created the following framework to help manage myself and others. My intent is that it will help you. The components are *Product, Process, Sources, Contacts, Initiative and Creativity*. Let's break them down.

Product

Each person in your organization must be clear on the product the company delivers to customers. Each member of the team must also understand that their role represents the product they deliver *to* the company. They need to know they have full latitude to fill that role to the very best of their ability. They need to know that they are responsible for being the absolute expert in what they do and that they will be expected to know more about their area of expertise than even their boss. When it appears that a problem is developing in their area, they have the obligation to bring that information to the attention of the leader along with potential options for what to do about it.

A good book on this concept is *The Great Game of Business* by Jack Stack. In this account, Jack describes how open book management enabled his team to exceed performance standards that appeared unachievable. The approach gave every employee visibility on how their work impacted the financial position of the company. With that insight, employees were able to develop and update processes that improved productivity and profitability. Which brings us to the next component…process.

Process

Simply defined, process is the way of doing things.

Process fits into categories that you can label. There are sales processes and production processes, hiring processes, and management processes. There are proven processes that you can adopt and adapt rather than creating them from scratch. That can only happen when tracking and documentation have defined the parameters of performance.

Processes should be written down and training programs created to teach them. An operations manual describes how each organizational component functions. Continuity books are more specific to a particular position in the organization. These documents set the basic standard. They do not restrict creative implementation. A person new to the job will be trained in the sales process based on what is outlined in the operations manual. As they get more experience, they may think they know a more effective way to get the sale; however, the manual will also outline how sales impact production, so the sales person knows not to oversell or make promises that the company cannot keep.

Each person in your organization must be clear on the overall process for getting products to market. Process helps them know how the work they do fits into the grand scheme of the company. If the process doesn't result in the desired outcome it will be the frontline people who have the best ideas on how to make adjustments. If employees are simply told to follow the process without deviation, they feel robbed of their ability to be creative and will allow your processes to deteriorate resulting in a negative effect on productivity. No process will be perfect and certainly not for any extended period of time. People who are forced to follow a broken process will eventually lose interest in trying to do the effective thing. They will do what they are told to do and let the chips fall where they may. They will leave it up to leadership to eventually realize the process failure by which time much opportunity may have been lost.

You can leverage the value of your employees by empowering them to seek alternative solutions when processes become ineffective. Better decisions can be made when everyone has an understanding of how the work flows. That doesn't mean that everyone goes rogue. It means that certain authority for change can be provided within boundaries and where the magnitude of a change proposal falls outside the authorized boundaries then the problem, with potential solutions, will be elevated to the leadership.

Process facilitates communication. Next to customer acquisition, communication is the most important aspect of building a successful company. When messages are not transmitted accurately and received effectively, the actions that result can rapidly derail a project. Instead of productive conversation, you have blame-casting, undermining, and back-stabbing. Process establishes who has responsibility for various aspects of a project. As your company grows, the levels of bureaucracy increase and messages are more prone to distortion. What must never be distorted is how the company functions. If employees are clear on how the process effects the product, they will recognize when a message has gotten garbled. If the culture provides a way for the frontline to voice their concerns, then operational mistakes can be avoided.

To improve processes, employees need to learn and grow with the company. They need to improve themselves not only in product knowledge, but in leadership ability. They will be a more valuable asset to the company if they are encouraged to identify sources and cultivate contacts, which we cover in the next two sections.

Sources

Using proven processes makes it easier to move forward fast. However, creating new processes takes time. Knowing where to look for proven processes is a process of its own. Sources include things that an employee can read, training programs that an employee can attend, or organizations that provide such options. Instead of looking for a new solution each time a recurring problem arises, it is more effective to identify a source that can shortcut the search. A source that has a proven ability to deliver will effectively streamline your operations. Here are some examples of sources:

- Procurement Technical Assistance Center (PTAC)
    - Guidance through the bid process
    - Websites, Registrations, Certifications
- Small Business Administration
    - Training
    - Loans
- Veterans Administration
    - Certifications
    - Opportunities
- SCORE
    - Consulting
    - Training
- GovCon Chamber of Commerce
    - Networking
    - Information

Inherent in a source is a person who has certain expertise or specialized knowledge. This is where contacts come in.

Contacts

Contacts are people. Pure and simple. They share what they know. They make connections with other people. Some contacts are more valuable than others. Encourage your employees to meet and cultivate relationships with the intent of growing their list of contacts. These relationships must be established early so these contacts are ready and willing to serve as trusted advisors or resource providers when the time comes. Contacts also include mentors and coaches, consultants, and counselors. A contact is not just any person. A contact is someone that can be relied on to get through a tough situation or out of a pinch. Employees need to understand where their contacts can make something happen and where they cannot. They must not abuse their contacts or they will lose them. They need to provide value in return or perhaps in advance to establish a trusted relationship.

You can help your employees by creating an environment that facilitates relationship building. Your employees can then build appropriate professional connections within that environment. Several relationships can facilitate the development of effective contacts: Strategic Alliances, Joint Ventures, sub-contracting, and teaming, among others. Here are some definitions:

- Strategic alliances - A strategic alliance is an *agreement* between two or more parties to pursue mutual objectives while remaining independent organizations. A strategic alliance is not a legal partnership.
- Joint ventures - A joint venture is a *business entity* created by two or more parties, generally characterized by shared ownership, shared risk and return, and shared governance. A joint venture is a legal partnership.
- Sub-contracting - A subcontractor is an individual or a business that signs a contract to perform part or all of the obligations of another's contract.
- Teaming - A teaming arrangement is formed when a prime contractor makes an agreement with one or more other companies to have them act as its subcontractors under a specified government contract.

Initiative

When your employees know the product, understand the process, and have cultivated sources and contacts, you can encourage them to take initiative. You can be confident that they will make the decisions that can be implemented at their level and bring the larger challenges to your attention, having already exhausted the easy answers. This will not only result in greater productivity, but will contribute to developing that difficult to acquire leadership experience. People don't learn responsibility unless they are given responsibility. You will trust them with the most challenging endeavors because you know they have the wherewithal to adapt and be resourceful when you can't provide them with resources.

Creativity

Management opens the door for creativity. You can be a more effective leader when you have an organization capable of working the details of your vision. Tapping into the creativity of everyone in the company leads to endless possibilities for growth. Harnessing the creativity of the team can be a tremendous help when environmental shifts dictate a need to pivot. Building such a team doesn't happen without intent.

Conclusion

How do you implement such a program? Here are five steps:

- **Product**: Work with your employees to elevate their expertise in the product the company delivers to customers and the product that they deliver to the company.
- **Process**: Discuss process on a regular basis, both with the entire team and with individuals. Include employees in process development and improvement. Continually seek ways that things can be done better. Demonstrate that you are interested and will implement good ideas.
- **Sources**: Connect employees with organizations that provide personal and professional development. Encourage them to document where they find the information most relevant to their areas of expertise.
- **Contacts**: Encourage each employee to list the people who have the knowledge and resources they rely on to do their jobs.
- **Initiative**: Hire employees that have an interest in helping your company grow. Support their suggestions to improve processes. Discuss the suggestions that may be more challenging to implement and make a good faith effort to understand the intent of the recommendation.
- **Creativity**: Implement an innovation program. Give everyone a means of submitting their ideas. Incentivize people for submitting ideas that get approved.

Having a management framework that everyone understands makes it possible to build and sustain a high performing team. If it happens that this particular framework does not appeal to you, I encourage you to create your own.

* * *

Colonel, US Air Force (retired) Dr. Russ Barnes is Chief Strategist for Systro Solutions, an organization development firm specializing in small business. He has more than 30 years' experience drawn from military service, small business ownership, executive coaching, strategy development and organization design consulting.

His Purposefully Profitable™ Program guides small business owners in creating and implementing a customized progression. In support of the Purposefully Profitable™ Program, he produced the Purposefully Profitable™ Podcast and the Mission Mapping™ Workshop. Russ speaks publicly on Organizing Your Business for Profitable Growth and CEO Skills for Small Business. He is the best-selling author of _Small Business for Service Members: 15 Things You Need to Know to be Purposefully Profitable_ and a co-author of two best-selling books: _Game Changers for Government Contractors_ and _Mission Unstoppable: Extraordinary Stories of Failures Blessings_.

Dr. Barnes received his Bachelor in Business Administration from Manhattan College (NY), his Master in Business Administration (MBA) from Embry-Riddle Aeronautical University, his Master of Science in Strategic Studies from Air University and his PhD in Organization Development from Benedictine University. The title of his dissertation is Organization Design for Small Business: A Discovery of Business Fundamentals for Executing a Purposeful Path to Profitability.

Connect with Russ by email - russ@systro.org or LinkedIn www.linkedin.com/in/rcbarnes.

For more information and education from Systro Solutions visit: https://www.systro.org/purposefully-profitable-program

Chapter 15.
Leading the Way

By Michael LeJeune

Partner at RSM Federal, Podcast Host – Game Changers for Government
Contractors

One of the guiding principles of my life is a simple phrase from Jim Rohn. *Never wish life were easier, wish you were better!* Today, this phrase goes through my mind every single time I get frustrated with anything in life.

Why is this such a powerful message? Because once you realize that life gets EASIER as YOU get better, getting better becomes your focus and it changes everything! Before this, it's easier to blame others, circumstances, the economy, the President, Democrats, Republicans, you name it. It's so easy to blame everyone but YOU for the challenges in your life.

So how does this apply to business? It's easy to blame your employees when revenue is down. It's easy to blame the job candidate pool when you just can't seem to "hire good people." It's also easy to blame "bad customers" when you have consistent challenges with them. It's HARD to realize how much responsibility you have for ALL of the above.

How does this apply to leadership? In your business, you are the leader. You set the tone. You set the direction. You are responsible for course correction when the ship slips even one degree off course. The team feeds off of your enthusiasm as well as your depression. And ultimately, the team learns to lead based on your example.

173

Another quote that guides my leadership mindset is that "Good leaders create leaders. Great leaders create leaders that create leaders." I have no idea who said that to me many years ago or I would quote them. But the impact of that statement has stuck with me for nearly 20 years. I'm not just thinking about the leaders I create. I'm thinking about the leaders that my leaders create. And if the formula is right, those leaders will continue to replicate this thinking and now we are talking about generations of leaders being built. That's an impact!

The Heart and Mind of a Leader

So where do you start? Regardless of where you rate yourself as a leader, a great place to look first is your heart and mind. It's very hard to separate the two. Our brains tend to look at how we "think" a leader should lead and that you have to be careful not to be too soft. Our heart typically wants to be nice or kind. Neither option is wrong. But it is a balancing act.

Here's an easy question. Now, it's just the two of us and I can't read your thoughts so please be honest. On a scale of 1 to 10 with 1 being the worst leader in the world and 10 being the best, where would you rate yourself? If you need to pause your reading for a minute to answer this, please do it. Where do you rate yourself?

Here's a follow-up question. Why did you rate yourself like that? Write your answers below. Why did you rate yourself the way you did?

Now, time for a softer question. What's one thing you could do to help take yourself from your current rating up to the next number? Write your answer below.

This is what it looks like to wish YOU were better! You put the focus on YOU and you take control of your destiny!

While we are on a roll, I'd like to ask you a few more questions. I've left a little space between questions for you write in your answer. It's important to get this information out of your head and on paper. If you want to find out what's in your head and your heart, write it down. If you don't want to write it down in fear that someone might read it, that's a good indication that you have some work to do. That's OK. We all do! It also provides you tremendous insight into the inner workings of your brain. Write it down and reflect on it.

What's your biggest challenge in your business and how do your leadership skills impact this challenge?

When you think of your employees, what's your first thought? Is it a good or bad thought and why?

Do you love your employees? If not, why?

How would you describe your relationship with your employees?

When you think of your customers, what's your first thought? Is it a good or bad thought and why?

Do you love your customers? If not, why?

How would you describe your relationship with your customers?

What are your aha moments from answering these questions?

If you haven't guessed it yet, in order to move forward, you have to understand your starting point. The previous questions should provide you with a very honest view of where you are. Don't be hard on yourself. Some of the best leaders in the world have devoted their entire lives to learning how to be a great leader and if you ask them to rate themselves today, they would probably only give themselves a solid 6 or 7.

I purposefully didn't tell you that YOUR scale should not be compared to the rating of other leaders. Your scale of 1 to 10 is based on where you are NOW against your POTENTIAL as a leader. This is why some of the best leaders only rate themselves a 6 or 7. They are rating themselves this way because they know they have the ability to improve.

Leadership by EXAMPLE is the hardest thing,
LEADERS DO! -Brian Woodall

Leadership is Contagious

At the beginning of this chapter I said that you set the tone in your business. What you may not realize is that you set the tone even when you are by yourself. Years ago my wife joined the multi-level-marketing company Premier Designs. We were just starting out in our business and this was a great way to make some extra money for our family.

It just so happened that the leader in my wife's up-line, Sandy Conway, was one of the biggest producers in the company. When she found out that I was a business coach, she asked me to speak at several of her events and their regional conference. As I was prepping to go on stage one night, Sandy got up to warm up the crowd. She said something that I never forgot. She said, "Your people don't do what you tell them to, they do what you do!" She expanded on this by explaining that it's not just what you do in public, it's also what you do in private.

You see, a leader's actions are so contagious that even when your people aren't around you, they are following your lead. You can't tell people what to do and not do it yourself. If you talk a big game but don't show up on the field, your people will see right through that.

Why is this? A better question is, how is this even possible? Believe it or not, your words and actions when you are with your team actually reveal a lot about what you do in private. If you are full of crap, your people will know it. Maybe not initially, but you can't hide it for long.

If all your employees ever see or hear from you is a lot of talk, and they don't see results, they will know that you don't practice what you preach. Why? Because you can't hide your results.

If you talk a big game and back it up with results, your people will see that too and they will follow your example.

Leadership is based on intent, purpose, and action.
Leadership is a great philosophy, but without action it's
nonexistent –Eric Baquol

The Top 3 Skills of a Business Leader

Skill #1: Knowing How to Ask Tough Questions

Curiosity in business is an asset. Regardless of what you may think, you don't know everything. For me, I'm always interested in learning something new. I'm just curious by nature. This means I'm always asking questions. I even ask questions when I think I know the answer. Even if I'm right, I could still learn something from one of my questions.

Questions, especially tough questions, allow other people on your team and in your network to participate. If you are the only one talking and you are only telling people what to do instead of asking them for their thoughts, you will eventually find yourself running a dictatorship that is 100% reliant on YOU to be RIGHT about everything. You don't want this. You want input and inclusion from your team and peers. You also want buy-in. It's very hard to get buy-in when every idea is yours and yours alone.

It's easy to ask softball questions. You know the kind. "What does everyone think?" or "Does anyone have anything they would like to add?" There's nothing wrong with asking these questions, but these are surface level questions that might not cut it in every situation. Let me give you an example.

About 20 years ago I worked for a small software company. I was the freshman director on our team, but I was the sales director. We were going through a product release review and someone called the product version 3.0. Our previous product version was 2.3. If you are not familiar with software development, going from a partial release (2.3) to a full new product release (3.0) is a significant increase. The market expects major improvement, added features, and some really cool bells and whistles.

During the product review, I learned that the development team was postponing several key features and was planning on massive improvements with a follow-up 3.1 release about three months after the 3.0 release. So I asked the tough question. "Why are we calling this release 3.0 instead of 2.5?" The room fell silent and then people started screaming at me. Remember, I was the freshman director. I was also half the age of most of the other directors. What could I possibly know?

Here were my follow-up thoughts to the team. I simply said, "If we release this as a major release without major features, our competitors will smell the blood in the water. Our customers will be pissed because they are required to do significant testing for every major release and our clients with classified systems need the patches in this release NOW. If we put out a release like this, we will also break our own description of what a major versus minor release is. Our integrity is on the line."

178

As you can imagine, this was not received very well from the team. I was openly attacked by almost every director on our team. We let everyone cool down for a few days and had a separate meeting with our CEO. He agreed with me and we changed the release version to 2.5. There's a lot more to this story that I don't have room for here, but I'll share this with you. Our customers repeatedly thanked me for doing this. They were going to have to jump through a lot of red tape to get a 3.0 version accredited for their networks in time for some very sensitive missions. The 2.5 release was what they needed and it was the most accurate.

Looking back on that experience, I still agree with what we did. I wish I would have asked the question sooner in the process and I wish I would have asked it a little differently. BUT and this is a big BUT, when our integrity was on the line, I asked some tough questions. I don't regret that.

In your business, the tough questions are usually the ones you know you need to ask, but don't necessarily want to. It could be a question about the direction of the company or why something IS or ISN'T working. You may need to ask a simple yet tough question for someone on your team like, "are you OK?" when you know they aren't. Sometimes it isn't the question that's tough, it's the answer on the other side. Ask it anyway.

Skill #2: Listening Skills

This is probably my favorite skill. Once you ask a question, especially a tough question, shut up! Don't talk over people. Don't interrupt them. Don't focus on your next answer. Just listen. This is not a complicated topic that requires 15 steps. Simply listen when people are talking and respond to what they said.

If you want to take your listening skills to the next level, I do have a trick for you. Get comfortable with silence. The average person can't stand silence. If you are in sales, you have probably been taught that once you make your pitch you are supposed to just shut up and let the prospect make up their mind. There's an old saying in sales that after the pitch, "the first person that talks loses." And in many cases, that's true. It's true because the first person that talks is usually on the defensive and in that moment, they are giving off a desperate vibe along with all of the power in the situation.

So how is this relevant in team meetings? If you are anxious to move on to the next question, you will skip over someone who wants and probably needs to speak. Just shut up and wait. This is NOT about power and control. This is about trust and giving people time to think. Not everyone thinks or acts at your pace. This is especially true if the topic is even remotely sensitive. Sometimes it takes a few seconds or even a minute for someone to gather their thoughts and get the courage to put those thoughts into words. Give them the time and the silence to do it.

Skill #3: The Ability to Drive Revenue

I know what you are probably thinking. Why is this one of your top three skills? As my partner Josh would say, "it's not about the money, it's about the money." At the end of the day, bringing in revenue solves a lot of problems in any business. Money pays yourself and your team. Money pays the bills. Money buys time. Without revenue, every little issue quickly becomes a raging bonfire and ultimately a distraction. While you may be in business to accomplish some philanthropic idea, you must drive revenue to make it happen. You can't fund anything with good thoughts and best wishes. You need money.

As a business owner, one of your key jobs is being able to drive revenue so that the company continues to move forward. That doesn't mean you have to pound the pavement and make the phone calls. It means that you have to know what levers to pull in your business to drive revenue. If you have a sales team, you need a close relationship with them. If you have a marketing team, you need a close relationship with them too.

My goal here is not to teach you everything there is to know about sales. My goal in this section is to highlight the importance of driving revenue and how that needs to be top-of-mind for you every single day in your business. You need to have your pulse on this at all times. In fact, I highly suggest you set up a sales dashboard to track this information and review it on a daily basis. If you stay focused on growing your revenue all other issues will seem minor and they won't distract you for your overall goals.

Your Biggest Asset as a Leader

Speaking of goals, your VISION as the leader of your company is without a doubt, the single biggest asset you have as a leader. A weak vision leads to you and your team just having a job. A job is something you do from 9 to 5 and you give it just enough effort to not get fired. A strong vision leads to a purpose. A purpose is something you think about all the time. You beat down barriers for a purpose. You go the extra mile for a purpose. A purpose is rewarding and fulfilling on both a financial and personal level. When you think about it in those terms, it makes it very clear how important your vision is.

You and your team need a common goal. Your vision is that goal. Whenever a distraction pops up and divides your team, your vision pulls you back together. A big, purposeful vision, is the backbone of your company.

With all of that said, most of the companies I speak with don't have a vision. Before I speak with a company, I always check their website. About half of the websites I review don't have any sort of vision or mission statement (which can be used interchangeably). About half of the websites I review have what I would call a mediocre vision. It's better than nothing, but not by much. It often looks a little something like "ABC consulting seeks to be the market leader in information technology." Does that look familiar to you? Is that similar to what you have on your website? Everyone wants to be a market leader. Maybe you already are a "leader" in your market. Now what? Does that inspire you or your team? Is it specific enough? How will you know when you are THE market leader in IT?

It's OK if you don't have a vision right now. It's OK if your vision is mediocre right now. You have the power to change that! You just need to make a commitment to creating a strong vision. The rest of this chapter is going to give you a framework for getting to that vision.

Key Elements of a Vision

Being Specific – It's really hard to hit a vague target. Your team needs a specific target that is easy to identify. This means no more saying, "We aim to be the best cybersecurity recruiting firm in the nation." How do you measure that? Here's one that's a bit more specific. "We aim to help 1,000,000 Veterans obtain a lucrative career in the cybersecurity industry." That may not be the best vision in the world, but it's specific, measurable, and to my next point, it's BIG!

BIG Vision – As you saw in the previous paragraph, being BIG is an essential part of your vision. Imagine for a minute if I had only written 100 or even 1,000 Veterans. That sounds nice, but it doesn't necessarily inspire your troops. A small vision feels more informal and like a short-term goal.

Think about that for a minute. What if you choose a small vision and hit it in your first couple of years? Then what? You just increase the number? Maybe you go back to the drawing board? Don't do this to yourself or your team. Think of a BIG LONG-TERM vision.

Your Rally Point – Creating a clear BIG vision is important, but one of the key pieces to making it a successful tool for your company is making sure that it can be a rally point for your troops. This typically means that your vision can't just be about money, market share, or some other business objective. Your employees will typically want some sort of philanthropic aspect of the vision. This allows them to get up every day with a purpose. It allows them to deal with setbacks as just that, a setback and not the end of the world. You and your employees will keep moving forward because it's not just about you and your families. It's about all of the lives you impact and good you do by accomplishing your vision. And that my friend, is easy to rally around.

Leveraging Your Vision

When your vision is clear, BIG, and a rally point for your employees, it also becomes a filter for your decisions. It attracts like-minded employees that are inspired to work for your company because it fulfills part of their own personal purpose. The right vision helps you decide which products and services you develop. If something doesn't fit with your vision, it sticks out like a sore thumb.

Always remember this phrase. *Your vision is a filter.* It's a filter for everything. That's why it needs to be powerful. You want a strong filter that will help guide your company to its destiny.

Finally, use your vision to set and track milestones. Let's take our example from above of 1,000,000 Veterans. That's a BIG number. The odds are not in your favor to hit that in year one. If you do hit that number in year one, please call me because I would like to work for you. LOL!

You can hit 1,000 Veterans in year one and maybe 2,500 in year two. As you develop your systems, you might be able to hit 10,000 in year three or four. My point is that your vision is your final objective, but there should be some attainable milestones along the way. This helps you know that you are moving in the right direction and helps your team know that these little milestones all add up.

I would recommend that you celebrate hitting each milestone. Don't wait until the vision is realized. You hit a milestone, you celebrate. You hit another milestone, you celebrate again!

Final Tips

Take your time with this. Your vision is important. It doesn't have to be perfect, but it also doesn't have to be rushed. If you don't know where to start, start with these simple questions. Why did you get into business? What were you hoping to accomplish? Most of the people I know that start their own business only did it for a couple of reasons. The most common reason is that they were tired of working for other people and wanted to control their own destiny. That's awesome. But what does that mean to you? Besides paying your own salary, what problem/s do you want to solve? That's another reason people start their own business. They see a problem in the market and they think their solution will cure it. These are all great reasons to start your own business.

Some people get into business with the focus of creating a lifestyle business. This means you likely don't want to have employee or maybe just a couple of 1099's. You don't have a bigger philanthropic goal or anything like that. You just want to build a business that funds your lifestyle. That's OK too. In that case, your vision is going to look a lot different. BIG for you might be owning a ranch in Montana on 100 acres and a vacation home in Florida. That's OK. I just want to urge you to get clear about that. When do you want to own it? Where in Montana and Florida? What are you going to do when you accomplish it?

Regardless of the size of your vision, your vision is important. I can say with first-hand experience that you will wake up one day (or a series of days) and want to quit your business. I've never met a business owner that hasn't had that feeling. When you have a bad day and nothing motivates you, your vision will refocus you and remind you of why you started your business. Use it to reenergize yourself and start fresh the next day!

* * *

Michael LeJeune is a bestselling author and master coach with RSM Federal. Michael hosts the wildly popular GovCon podcast **Game Changers**

for Government Contractors, manages the **Federal Access Platform**, and specializes in helping GovCon business owners brand themselves as Subject Matter Experts in their niche.

Michael and his business partner Joshua Frank have helped their GovCon clients win over $2.8 billion in government contracts and more than 30+ billion in IDCs. Over 1,000 Government contractors trust the Federal Access Platform as their primary source for GovCon education, training, coaching, and practical strategies for winning government contracts.

Federal Access Platform for GovCon
Get more than 300 essential documents and templates, 100+ training videos, and industry leading Subject Matter Expertise (SME) to accelerate your government sales. You can start your journey with us today for $29 by visiting https://federal-access.com/govconexpertsbook

---

Chapter 16.
Authentic Leadership

By Emily Harman

Founder of The Onward Movement, President of Emily Harman Coaching and Consulting

Embark on a Quest of Self Discovery

You've retired from military service or you've decided to leave active duty and you're figuring out what to do next. As Veterans, when we leave military service, we typically retire outright, work for a company, or work for ourselves. Making a decision on what to do after leaving active duty requires understanding yourself. Understanding yourself requires deep introspection and takes time.

No matter what you choose to do after leaving military service, it's a good idea to take a pause and make sure you understand yourself and *why* you're choosing your next step. Taking time to reimagine yourself as a retiree, an employee, or a veteran business owner, takes courage and self-introspection.

Let My Story Help You Remember Yours

Perhaps you can relate to aspects of my story. I made a decision at age 17 to attend the U.S. Naval Academy. After graduation, I served on active duty for 7 years, then became a civil servant and retired from civil service in May 2019. I also served in the Navy reserves for 13 years.

185

Upon deciding to retire from my civil service career with the Navy, I received solicited and unsolicited advice on what I *should* do next. You *should* work for a large government contractor. You *should* work for a small business supporting the federal government. You *should* start a small business in support of the federal government. You *should* be a consultant for government contractors.

I also received advice on what I *should not* do. You *should not* retire - you're too young. You *should not* retire - you will get depressed with nothing to do. You *should not* retire - you should go for the next promotion.

Let Go of the "Shoulds"

It was at this point that I decided I was going to do what *I* wanted to do, not what others thought I *should* do. I decided to let go of the "shoulds" and create a lifestyle on my terms. Interested in doing the same? Keep reading this chapter. Also, check out my Onward Podcast interview with Manuj Aggarwal. All Onward Podcast episodes are available here: https://emilyharman.com/onwardpodcast/

Manuj is an entrepreneur, investor, and CTO of TetraNoodle. TetraNoodle is a software consulting company that helps startup founders with tech projects. Manuj started his career at the age of 15, working in a factory for twelve hours a day, six days a week, earning a cool $2 per day. While building his career, Manuj fought decades of anxiety, depression, and pessimism. He did this by indulging in meditation and mindfulness. Manuj and I discuss many things in this interview; however, one of my biggest takeaways is in the title of the episode: Let Go of "Shoulds" and Live *Your* Life!

I was ready to let go of the "should." But what did I want to do? After raising children while working, mostly as a single parent, I had always put others first. I didn't really know myself. I hadn't taken time to dream. After working for the Navy for 38 years, I knew I wanted to create a life on my terms. Who was I? What did I want? I didn't even know.

The Inner Work of Self-Discovery

I took steps to discover *my* answers to these questions. I started to do the inner work and I've learned the most valuable tool: how to listen to the guidance of my Inner Voice, my Higher Self, my Authentic Self.

I created a roadmap for an authentic and fulfilling life. I'm still on my journey of self-discovery. If you're a lifelong learner like me - the journey never ends! Now I'm living a life I'd never before imagined. I'm pursuing my dreams with confidence and living life on *my* terms. And I get to help others do the same.

Quest for Leading an Authentic Life

Brené Brown, a research professor at the University of Houston, best-known for her famous TED talk, "The Power of Vulnerability," says "Authenticity is a collection of choices that we have to make every day. It's about the choice to show up and be real. The choice to be honest. The choice to let our true selves be seen."

In working for the military, I didn't always feel I could show up and be real and I lost connection with my true self somewhere along the way. As part of living life on my terms, I decided to create a podcast. I published the first seven episodes of the Onward Podcast in June 2019. Since then, I've interviewed over 100 guests! Each guest shares invaluable insight into how to lead an authentic life.

In one of my first Onward Podcast episodes entitled *Be Your Authentic Self - Even When the Law Says You Can't,* my Naval Academy classmate, Zoe Dunning, shares the obstacles she faced when she came out as lesbian while serving in the military. We also discuss her successful challenge to the military's Don't Ask, Don't Tell policy. Zoe is the first and only openly gay person allowed to remain on active duty in the military prior to the end of the Don't Ask, Don't Tell policy. I admire Zoe for her authenticity, courage, and leadership during such a difficult time of intense public scrutiny.

After I retired, I conducted more Onward Podcast interviews and continued my self-discovery process. As I shared my self-discovery journey with others, I realized I wasn't alone. I talked with transitioning veterans, civil servants, men, women, business owners, retirees, who realized they too wanted to embark on their own journey of self-discovery.

I founded the Onward Movement and developed a roadmap, a framework to enable others to bravely embrace authenticity and release the fear of judgment so they can pursue their dreams with confidence. You can join the Onward Movement here:
https://www.facebook.com/groups/onwardmovement

As members of the Onward Movement, we affectionately refer to ourselves as Onwarders. We interact mainly in the Facebook group, but we also support each other in online training and networking sessions, book discussions, and in-person retreats. The Onward Movement is a compassionate community and a safe place to connect and engage with other Onwarders. You'll find access to tools, resources, and support for each step of your journey.

Develop a Mindset for Personal Transformation

I update the Onward roadmap based on my transformation journey as I gain more knowledge and insight. You can go through your transformational journey by yourself, by reading books, watching videos, and using what you find searching the internet.

If you want to accelerate your self-discovery process and quest for creating your authentic life, I highly recommend investing in a personal coach. Ideally, you should choose a coach who has been through the journey themselves and someone with whom you trust. Also, I recommend investing in a personal coach who invests in themselves. In other words, a coach who has a coach. If you'd like to learn more about my Onward Accelerator Coaching Program, please schedule a complimentary personal coaching session from my website www.emilyharman.com.

Mindset for Your Personal Transformation Journey

The personal transformation process shouldn't be rushed. It's scary. It's messy. It's emotionally challenging. Feelings you did not know you had will come up. Sometimes you may feel like you're going backwards. During the process, you'll figure out how to go forward, to move onward. And....it's worth it!

Before embarking on your self-discovery journey, it's important to develop a mindset for personal transformation. Make sure you know *your* why. Why are you embarking on this journey? Are you ready to leave your comfort zone? Reflect upon times when you've left your comfort zone in the past. What did you learn about yourself?

Become aware of and learn how to tame the voice of your inner critic. We all have one. One strategy is to make a list of the things your inner critic regularly tells you. Some of these may sound familiar: "I can't do this." I don't know anything about business." "Who am I to start my own business?" "It's too late for me to make changes in my life." "I'm not good at keeping promises to myself." "What if someone figures out I'm an imposter?"

What does your inner critic say? Write it down and then write the responses you'll give your inner critic when you hear her/him say these things to you.

Expect to do some deep introspection. You'll examine your beliefs, your thoughts, your feelings, and your reactions when others judge you. You'll learn to let go of buried thoughts and emotions keeping you from being authentic in all aspects of your personal and professional lives.

Discover Your Purpose

I recommend embarking on this journey even if you already know what you want to do when you leave military service. You will improve your self-awareness, discover or confirm your purpose, own your journey, and believe in yourself.

Part of this journey entails soul searching, exploring your past, and discovering, or rediscovering your passions. You may discover, as Onward Podcast guest Dave Sanderson learned, one defining moment can create a lifetime of purpose.

When US Airways Flight 1549, otherwise known as "The Miracle on the Hudson", "crashed" into the Hudson River in January 2009, Onward Podcast guest Dave Sanderson survived. Consequently, he started to realize that the moments that made up his life prepared him for that moment. Thinking only of helping others, Dave became the last person off of the back of the plane that day. Furthermore, he was largely responsible for making sure others made it out safely.

An inspiring survivor, Dave was an ordinary person in an extraordinary situation. Sharing the lessons of that day with audiences around the world, he shows that managing your state of mind and leading with certainty can turn anyone into a hero. In this episode, Dave talks about how to step up and lead yourself through adversity.

In addition, he believes one defining moment can create a lifetime of purpose. Dave speaks about *Point in Time That Changes Everything* (PITTChE). Finally, everyone has a PITTChE moment. Find yours, focus on adding value to others first, and watch how your life takes off.

Develop Self-Awareness

Authentic leaders are self-aware. They're willing to get curious, to listen and challenge their assumptions. This starts with understanding your unique story as you chart your own course in creating the next phase of your life. Knowing your uniqueness enables you to communicate from a place of authenticity, ultimately making you a better person, father, wife, husband, partner, parent, employee, business owner, community leader, etc.

Set time aside every day for reflection. Daily journaling is an excellent exercise to increase your awareness. Make it a habit to write three pages a day. You'll be amazed at the results. Need help thinking of what to write? The internet is full of journaling prompts to help you get started.

As an entrepreneur, you may discover you get so focused on your business that other aspects of your life suffer. From time to time this is understandable. It's not realistic to be in perfect balance all of the time. However, it's not sustainable. Part of your journey should entail assessing all aspects of your life, finances, personal/spiritual growth, relationships, health and wellbeing, recreational time, in addition to running your business.

The self-awareness and knowledge you'll gain along this journey is life changing. It will give you confidence and enable you to be an even more authentic leader. Your authenticity will be visible to others. They'll feel it. They'll see it in your being. Your authenticity will give others permission to be authentic as well.

You'll find your customers, employees, family members, and others in your network will respond positively to your authentic vibe. You'll earn trust and respect. All areas of your life will improve.

You'll know your strengths and weaknesses and let go of habits that no longer serve you and develop new habits. You'll get better at setting boundaries and to saying no without feeling guilty. Your business will benefit too. If you know yourself and you lead a company, you'll hire people who compliment your strengths and fill your gaps.

Your Choices Shape Your World

Imagine where you'll be one year, three years from now, after you embark on your journey of self-discovery. What will happen in your life, both personally and professionally?

As part of your personal transformation journey, I recommend you listen to my Onward Podcast episodes with Sky Nelson-Isaacs. Sky is a physicist, educator, speaker, musician, and author. We discuss living in flow in the episode entitled *The Science of Synchronicity and How Your Choices Shape Your World*. Sky uses real life examples to show how our choices shape our world. What choices will you make to shape your world?

In the episode entitled *A Scientific Mechanism for Being in the Right Place at the Right Time*, Sky presents a scientific mechanism for synchronicity. Every day, with synchronicities as stepping stones, life experiences are calling you forth toward a greater sense of fulfillment and accomplishment. Furthermore, each of us in our own way walks through life asleep to our power to create change.

Listen to this episode and learn how living in flow helps us stop repeating stubborn patterns of experience. Learn how you can discover choices you're making which may be having undesirable consequences. Furthermore, learn how you can change unconscious opinions or feelings that are getting in your way. Finally, when you become aware of ways that you want your behavior to change, you can accomplish that change more quickly and more lastingly.

Your choices shape *your* world. What are you waiting for?

Here are some additional resources to help you with your journey.

- Onward Movement Roadmap
  https://tinyurl.com/onwardroadmap
- Onward Movement Manifesto
  https://tinyurl.com/onwardmanifesto
- Join the Onward Movement for FREE by visiting:
  https://www.facebook.com/groups/onwardmovement

- Schedule a free call with Emily to learn more about her Onward Accelerator Coaching Program:
https://calendly.com/emilyharman/15min

* * *

Emily Harman has 38 years of service to her country as both a Naval Officer and civilian, retiring as a member of the Senior Executive Service in May 2019. A trailblazer, Emily was in the sixth class of women to graduate from the U. S. Naval Academy. Commissioned a Supply Corps Officer, Emily was one of the first two officers on the U.S.S, Emory S. Land, AS-39 to qualify as a Supply Corps Surface Warfare Officer. Recognized as a role model, Emily served as a Company Officer and Leadership Instructor at the Naval Academy.

As a Department of the Navy (DON) civilian, Emily served as a Contracting Officer for professional services and major weapons systems in support of Naval Aviation. Her last assignment was Director of the Department of the Navy's Office of Small Business Programs where she served as the chief advisor to the Secretary of the Navy on all small business matters.

Upon retirement, Emily founded the Onward Movement which seeks to inspire at least 10,000 people to embrace authenticity and release the fear of judgment so they can pursue their dreams with confidence. She guides her clients on a path to lead an authentic and fulfilling life through her Onward Accelerator Coaching Program. Emily also hosts the Onward Podcast featuring authentic conversations on facing adversity and moving forward.

Emily received a B.S. in Physical Science from the U.S. Naval Academy and a M.S. in Acquisition and Contract Management from the Florida Institute of Technology.

Connect with Emily on LinkedIn:
https://www.linkedin.com/in/emily-harman-cpcm-8580413/

Chapter 17.
Fulfilling Your Promises (Product Development for the Purpose of Doing Business with the Government)

By Russ Barnes

Founder, Systro Solutions

Money is the reward for risks taken, value delivered, and promises kept. – Robin Sharma

Whether you are looking to land an initial government contract or add lines of business by pursuing contracts in the government sector, the product development process provides an intentional way of establishing a lucrative business relationship with the government. If you haven't put your value into a package that can be purchased with a price, you will experience anxiety every time the question of how much you charge comes up.

Your value may be crystal clear to you, but if it isn't packaged as a product, you will never make a sale. Value is intangible. Solutions are conceptual. You can't sell value or a concept until you put it into a form that can be assessed, compared against alternatives and purchased.

Product is made up of three components – solution, package, and price. A product is something you can put a label on. You can describe it in a word. You can tell people what it is without a long explanation about what it does. People can either see it or visualize it.

Product development is about shaping something valuable for people to purchase with a way for them to pay. Sounds simple and it is, but often we are not able to clearly describe what we're selling. If you have a widget, it's easy to talk about the features and benefits, but features and benefits don't always indicate how the product solves a problem in a way that saves money, makes money, or saves time. If the consumer does not see how your product will make their life better, then they are not likely to purchase. So, it is imperative that you view your product from the perspective of the customers you prefer to attract.

Developing a product is a captivating process that can lead to obsession. Some business owners spend so much time perfecting their product that they forget the point is to solve a real problem for a real person.

Your product is what gives your company value. Your product should be created in a way that anyone can sell it on your behalf. If your product is you, your scalability will be limited. You will have to trade hours for dollars until you can create passive forms of income based on your status as a celebrity.

Everything you do in business is tied to the product. Ordinarily, products don't sell themselves. Having a great product doesn't mean people will beat down your door. In practice, many people do hope that, if they develop an attractive enough product, they won't have to sell it.

Once you have clarity on your value and have identified the problem that you want to solve you need to express it in the form of a product that the government can purchase. A product framed in the form of a package can then be priced appropriately.

The government procurement process forces you to do this. The government is seeking solution providers, just like everybody else. You have to let them know that you have a solution they will love. If you lack clarity on how you can help the government solve a problem, then you won't know which contracts make sense for your company. You will submit bids for the opportunities that appear easy to win or that you think you can fulfill or perhaps you will choose the contracts that pay a lot of money with the intent that you will figure out how to meet the requirements once you close the deal. If this is how you approach this game, you may be the type of person who is comfortable with jumping from an airplane and building your parachute on the way down...metaphorically speaking. Exciting for sure, but your chances of smashing unimpeded into the earth at a high rate of speed is a strong possibility. Savvy business owners strap on a parachute before they jump.

Fortunately, the government provides a procurement process parachute of sorts. NAICS codes are a list of products and services the government purchases. The North American Industry Classification System (NAICS) is used to classify industries. You can either identify a product on this list of things the government buys and find a way to provide it or you can research how much the government buys of your current product or service and pursue those contracts.

The government does not give handouts. It has requirements which demand quality solutions. Every contract is competed in one way or another. Even in the case of a GSA award, there are other companies on the same GSA schedule who have the opportunity to be selected for the contract award. Since there are typically a large number of companies competing for the most lucrative contracts, the government will find as many ways as possible to eliminate candidates and reduce the number of profiles they have to review.

The government is an entity, but within that entity are real people making the contract award decisions. The government can't make or produce everything it needs to function. The people who are charged with making purchases to fill those needs are known as contracting officers and it's their job to get the best solutions. In that sense, there is risk involved. The contracting officer has to trust you to deliver on the requirements in full and you have to trust the government to make a fair deal and pay you when the job is done.

Therefore, it's important that you communicate to this government official how well you can meet his/her need. If you are an experienced business owner, you have past performance as proof. If you are new to business, you will need something else that indicates you have the ability to fulfill the contract.

There are five steps to preparing your product so that you consistently fulfill your promises and develop a solid record of past performance. They are 1) Identify the problem, 2) Match your solution, 3) Package the solution as a program, 4) Price the program appropriately, and 5) Present the package competitively. Let's break them down:

Identify the Problem

Understand what problems the government needs to solve and whether your company has the skills and resources to solve those problems. The government presents its problem in the form of Requests for Proposals (RFPs). RFPs are one of the vehicles the government uses to solicit bids.

Imagine your unique set of solutions. The Small Business Administration is a source of information that you can use to match your solutions to government needs and make sure you have or can acquire the resources to fulfill the requirements. This website provides a way to evaluate your readiness: https://www.sba.gov/federal-contracting/contracting-guide/assess-your-business.

Matching Solutions

Matching solutions to problems by category is a way to determine the forms your product might take. For example, if the problem is physical and falls into the category of health (see below), viable solutions include nutrition and exercise programs. You can offer a solution in the nutrition sub-category that might take the form of a menu, a diet program, a supplement, a meal, or a philosophy, among other things. You might also offer a solution in the exercise sub-category that takes the form of a physical training program or a book about running or weight lifting or plyometrics. The product package you choose should be suited to your expertise. Below are some problem/solution combinations listed with an associated product package in parentheses.

- Physical problems
    - Health (nutrition and exercise programs)
    - Productivity (devices, tools and templates)
- Psychological problems
    - Knowledge (educational programs)
    - Trauma (counseling sessions)
    - Decision making (Coaching programs)
- Financial Problems
    - Career (job search, staffing services)
    - Entrepreneur (business development programs)
    - Investor (funding options)

Package the Chosen Solution

You must be good at effectively describing the way your company solves problems. Terminology and language are key parts of the packaging process. You might have the best solution on the planet, but if your description is difficult to understand, it will not sell. The government helps you by providing terminology and language in the NAICS codes mentioned earlier. Using their language to describe your solutions will increase your ability to communicate your value. Based on NAICS, the following categories represent the most opportunity:

NAICS codes (Top 6)

- Code 54: Professional Scientific Tech Services - 2.3 million businesses
- Code 81: Other Services - 1.9 million businesses
- Code 44-45: Retail Trade - 1.8 million businesses
- Code 62: Health Care - 1.7 million businesses
- Code 56: Waste Management and Remediation Services - 1.6 million businesses
- Code 23: Construction - 1.5 million businesses

Price the Package

To set your pricing appropriately requires research. It helps to find out how much the government has paid for various products and services in the past. That information is readily available and is critical to submitting a competitive bid.

There are ways to identify how much the government has paid for products and services in the past. The GSA E-Library is one source for such research. You can also sit down with your local Procurement Technical Assistance Center to walk through the proposals that interest you. Here are some sites that you will find useful in your research:

- http://fptac.org/six-step-gateway/
- https://www.sba.gov/business-guide/grow-your-business/get-more-funding
- https://beta.sam.gov/help/wage-determinations

If you already have a pricing model that you use with non-government clients, then you know your margins and can evaluate government opportunities to see if any of them fit your profit model. Be prepared to accept the fact that the government sector may not be an option because the opportunities for profit are not there for a company of your size. On the other hand, there may be value in doing business with the government, even if you can only achieve breakeven, because it keeps your people employed during cycles where your more lucrative commercial contracts are slow. It may also give you the opportunity to develop a track record with the government that positions you for more profitable contracts in the future. This where you put on your strategic thinking cap and consider all avenues.

Present the Package

Your presentation plays as much of a role as your product in winning a contract. The procurement proposal process is daunting. Make no mistake. There is nothing easy about it. If every "i" is not dotted and every "t" is not crossed in accordance with directions, the proposal will be rejected before it is even looked at for consideration on its merits.

A capability statement is a standard marketing document that provides a snapshot of your company. It tells the government what you do and how well you've done it in the past. Your past performance is the proof that you can do what you say you can do. It also gives you the opportunity to highlight your differentiators. Those differentiators include: Service-Disabled Veteran Owned Small Business (SDVOSB), Minority Business Enterprise (MBE) or Woman Owned Business Enterprise (WBE) among a myriad of others.

You might also put together a set of slides that go into detail about your company. Within this presentation, you will want to answer questions that are frequently asked, such as:

- How will you deliver the results you've promised?
- How many people will be involved?
- How much material will be required?
- How long will it take to complete the project?
- How long will normal processes be disrupted before the project is complete?
- What will the organization look like after changes have been made?

- How extensive will the changes be and how will they impact jobs and money?
- In your proposal you want to give the evaluator the ability to envision a satisfactory outcome.

Conclusion

Be thoughtful about your product development. To compete well, focus is a key to providing a quality solution. People want to buy the best. No one asks for the second-best provider. Here are five steps to creating a product you can be proud of:

1) Identify the problem
2) Match your solution
3) Package the solution as a program
4) Price the program appropriately
5) Present the package competitively

* * *

Colonel, US Air Force (retired) Dr. Russ Barnes is Chief Strategist for Systro Solutions, an organization development firm specializing in small business. He has more than 30 years' experience drawn from military service, small business ownership, executive coaching, strategy development and organization design consulting.

His Purposefully Profitable™ Program guides small business owners in creating and implementing a customized progression. In support of the Purposefully Profitable™ Program, he produced the Purposefully Profitable™ Podcast and the Mission Mapping™ Workshop. Russ speaks publically on Organizing Your Business for Profitable Growth and CEO Skills for Small Business. He is the best-selling author of Small Business for Service Members: 15 Things You Need to Know to be Purposefully Profitable and a co-author of two best-selling books: *Game Changers for Government Contractors* and *Mission Unstoppable: Extraordinary Stories of Failures Blessings.*

Dr. Barnes received his Bachelor in Business Administration from Manhattan College (NY), his Master in Business Administration (MBA) from Embry-Riddle Aeronautical University, his Master of Science in Strategic Studies from Air University, and his PhD in Organization

Development from Benedictine University. The title of his dissertation is Organization Design for Small Business: A Discovery of Business Fundamentals for Executing a Purposeful Path to Profitability.

Connect with Russ by email - russ@systro.org or LinkedIn (www.linkedin.com/in/rcbarnes).

For more information and education from Systro Solutions visit: https://www.systro.org/purposefully-profitable-program

Chapter 18.
From Kitchen to Conference Room: Growing Your Solopreneurship Beyond Yourself

By Eric "Doc" Wright, PhD

Founder, Vets2PM

Introduction

A primary component of any business size classification schema is Employee Count (EC). Generally, businesses with less than 500 employees are considered 'small' and according to the US Small Business Administration (SBA), there are 30.7 million small businesses in the US, which account for 99.9% of all US businesses.[19] Additionally, businesses with 10 employees or less are generally considered a Small Office/Home Office (SOHO).[20]

That's who this chapter is primarily for, the solopreneur, perhaps you, siting at your kitchen table or home office right now reading this, trying to figure out how to scale your business beyond yourself. You may want to do this for several reasons; such as increasing profitability, productivity, or performance. Or, to develop a team of responsible, accountable, capable people you can delegate roles and tasks to so you can continue to grow the

---

[19] http://bit.ly/2019SmallBusinessProfile
[20] http://bit.ly/WhatIsAnSMEBusiness

business. Or, to make a larger economic or legacy impact by employing more folks, to serve more folks, to create more economic activity. Or, because you feel your business fulfills some existing need and your goods and services are the answer.

Regardless of the reason, I can tell you after coaching hundreds of primarily solopreneur small businesses and supporting many mid-to-large ones, that right-sized staffing is a constant challenge. However, it is a critical one that must be handled successfully if you are to grow and flourish at whatever growth stage your business is in. In fact, this is what my company specializes in, helping government contractors meet the challenges of expanding and contracting staff rapidly to reduce the uncertainty and carrying costs inherent in growing a business.

There are massive labor costs to carrying a staff large enough to staff any award you may win. They aren't sustainable. Additionally, there is massive uncertainty if you don't! What happens if you win an award and need 27, or 54, or 235 employees for that federal contract you just won...and you only have five weeks because that's when the contract starts? That's risky! Will those employees be available and be ready to initiate the contact? The answer is likely unknown.

When I speak with clients, growing their organizations beyond themselves is usually in the conversation somewhere, and this milestone is usually somewhere on their future timeline. A model I use to provide them perspective and context is James Fischer's Seven Stages of Growth model. [21] It is simple, extremely informative, comprehensive, and exceptionally practical. In fact, it is so powerful, it is required reading in my company. I expect my executive management team and mangers to understand it and its application, so we all pull the rope in the same direction.

Basically, over a 6 year period, James interviewed 650 entrepreneurial CEOs and uncovered the relationship between employee count (EC), capabilities, impacts, outcomes, complexities, challenges, and leadership for each leader and his or her company's managers; understanding what needs to be in each stage to sustain and benchmark business growth.[22] EC is a

---

[21] http://bit.ly/CheatSheetForGrowthCurve

fundamental hallmark of each growth stage: 1-10 employees is stage one (statistically, likely you as you read this); stage two is 11-19 employees (again, statistically you, if you're not in the previous category); stage three is 20-34 employees; stage four, 35-57 employees; stage five 58-95 employees; stage six has 96-160 employees; and stage seven is 161-500 employees.

So, this chapter is for you solopreneur! I share it with you to help you grow your business. It's for those working from the kitchen table to your high-performing team, to your business' board room. This can be a really challenging task, and one that most solopreneurs struggle with. It covers growing your team beyond yourself to your first 9 employees. It also highlights what you should stay focused on and some of the challenges you should prepare for as you grow into stage two, such as 'watch your cash,' 'hire for person-company fit,' and 'provide and solicit feedback often to build trust and autonomy,' all to help you focus and grow. First trick, once you realize which stage you are in, and each time thereafter, start focusing really hard on the next stage. Develop the capabilities and characteristics of that next stage.

I have created thousands of successful, high-performing executive-level teams in projects across the private, public, and government sectors through my own successful multi-million dollar company Vets2PM.[23] My company is a nationally recognized 501(c)3 that I co-founded with Joe Pusz of the PMO SQUAD, as well as supporting the Veteran Project Manager Mentor Alliance ("VPMMA"),[24] and dozens of small veteran-owned businesses ("VOB") I have coached over the years with the Florida Association of Veteran Owned Businesses ("FAVOB").[25] Let's see if we can't help you do the same.

Culture

First, we'll start with the bedrock to build your team and business on, your culture. It is critical to everything that will flow from it. Then we'll

---

[22] https://www.igniteyourbiz.com/7-stages-of-growth.shtml
[23] https://vets2pm.com/
[24] https://www.thevpmma.org/
[25] https://favob.net/

discuss how to assemble your high-performing team (HPT). Finally, we'll conclude with how to coach and empower your HPT to its fullest performance potential. Let's dive into culture!

The culture you create will directly influence your team's future behavior, decision-making, productivity, and performance, which will ultimately influence your profitability and longevity. Every day. Even when you're not around. A strong cultural presence will be paramount to your success in building and maintaining an HPT, including a capability of scaling through concentric rings of employees that you'll add.

But what is culture? In my mind, and in my organizations, it is the combination of our mission, vision, values, and processes, which in turn drives our decision-making, behavior, and performance. These components have become so ubiquitous in today's workplace that they are often underrated, underappreciated, and dare I say, in some instances, cliché. In fact, many of these hang on walls and halls across corporate America as empty platitudes! This is unfortunate. And costly!

In fact, the late, great management guru Peter Drucker said, "culture eats strategy for breakfast!" I'll illustrate what he meant using how I've built it into Vets2PM. And why it matters!

At Vet2PM, our corporate culture is the result of our deep conviction for, and commitment to our mission, process, values, standards, our veteran clients, corporate America customers, and our great Nation's government and economy.

We help military veterans achieve meaningful, lucrative post-service intra or entrepreneur careers (*mission*); using our knowledge, skills, and decades of experience to: 1) Inspire them with a clear, meaningful, lucrative end-state as a career Project Manager or Veteran-Owned Business owner; 2) Train them to deliver project success and obtain in-demand project management credentials; 3) Prepare them for reintegration into the civilian workforce, i.e. the civilian division (CIVDIV) with professional resumes, interview skills, LinkedIn profile creation or make-overs, and social media savvy; and 4) Place them into meaningful, lucrative project, program, and general management careers for life (*process*)...with integrity, commitment, and excellence in everything we do (*values*). These values include:

1. Integrity: our communications and interactions with others are always truthful, transparent, timely, and clear.

2. Commitment: we always keep our commitments to our veteran customers, corporate and government clients, teaming partners, teammates, processes and systems, and company image and culture.

3. Excellence: we constantly demonstrate responsibility, accountability, and ownership for all timely, accurate work products and services we produce (*standards*)".

So as you can see above, we have laid down an example of our mission, vision, values, and process. How do we use it? What is its impact?

Well, we couple these components with a clear, well-communicated decision-making criterion for team members. This compilation becomes our doctrine; how we behave in congruence with growing the company's mission. Now that newly arriving team members know what we believe, and why and how deeply we believe it, we can show them what we value and use these components holistically to make decisions congruent with growing that value, along with a growing team delivering it. This all serves to allow us to hire and develop responsible, accountable, capable folks we can delegate to, with confidence, to achieve the desired results, which is a necessity to grow.

Continuing our Vets2PM illustration, our decision-making criteria is clear and consistently applied. First, we ask "Does this help us help military veterans achieve meaningful, lucrative, post-service intra or entrepreneur careers?" This ensures we keep our eyes on the mission and its ultimate litmus test, serving our customers through their success. First, it answers the question "what are we doing?"

Next, we ask, "How will we know if it has helped us help military veterans achieve meaningful, lucrative, post-service intra or entrepreneur careers?" This answer becomes our program or project's Key Performance Indicator (KPI). It's the "how well are we doing it/did we do it?" answer.

Then we ask, "what do we need to pull it off?" This includes scoping, scheduling, budgeting and financing, and identifying performance standards and service levels. It allows us to not only develop the product or service, but to also plan its implementation and operationalization. A plan is only successful if it is implemented and we achieve what we planned to achieve. There has to be some proof to the pudding!

Finally, we discuss how the consideration exhibits our values of integrity, commitment, and excellence. Our values are overtly discussed, so we can answer the mail successfully, as that's how we'll judge the ultimate outcome. Did we help military veterans achieve meaningful, lucrative post-service intra or entrepreneur careers with integrity? Why? Because it's the right thing to do and helps our customers and clients succeed. Commitment, we can deliver successfully and consistently to meet expectations. And excellence, the results delivered meet or exceed shared expectations to enhance the customer or client's position.

This collection of clearly stated concise items serves to collectively guide our individual word, deed, and decision-making. This is all independent of the founder! This facilitates delegation, which means growth beyond yourself!

You have now established your company's doctrine! You are on your way to company longevity, independent of you! And speaking of doctrine, I'd encourage you check out some of the amazing work by Mark Bonchek, PhD, over at SHIFTthinking.[26]

Initial Nine Team Members

Now that your culture is set, you're ready to begin bringing ownership-minded team members onboard. "Why ownership minded folks Doc?" you may ask. Well, frankly, they steward the business, care for the company's customers, clients, and reputation; they give a bit more than the minimum effort necessary every day to get a pay check; they choose only projects and programs that serve the market well by generating value and revenue; and they spend money like it's their own. They don't mail it in. They exceed the standards. They are responsible, accountable, capable individuals. They run the company like it's theirs!

---

[26] http://bit.ly/LettingGoWithoutLosingControl

You probably have surmised by now that one of your initial challenges to growing the company beyond yourself are 1) your ability to delegate, and 2) your personnel's capability to accept it. Delegation is tricky. Can you learn to do it? Can you learn to do it well? And, can the personnel you hire accept it? Can they accept it well? Are they responsible, accountable, creative, resilient, and capable?

What does this mean? It means that you have to have a clear process and system for deciding what to delegate, to whom to delegate based on their strengths, personality, and capabilities, and clear expectations about what meeting the delegated task/item/goal means. Me? I do it like this. "Is what I'm doing right now contributing to growth through team member development, teaming, revenue generation, developing future products or services, and developing or nurturing beneficial relationships?" Also, "Am I the only one capable of doing this?" I ask these questions of myself, in this order. It keeps me focused on my role of growing the company.

Now, to the team members. Your early stage responsibilities encompass establishing team member roles and functions, setting performance expectations and criteria, and developing behavioral questions to screen for an ownership mindset, adaptability, responsibility, and accountability so that you place a team around you that is full of folks that you can delegate to. And they can deliver. Consistently. So, that you grow your team and company beyond yourself!

First, let's start with the end in mind. Think about your business and its needs depending on which stage you're in. Review Fischer's Seven Stage Growth model for the characteristics, tools, and capabilities you want to develop.[27] Use these thoughts to craft questions aimed at uncovering how the candidate would behave in certain situations. These situations represent the ethics, values, beliefs, adaptability, responsibility, accountability, and decision-making situations you commonly encounter in your business. You're trying to uncover how they will behave when you're not looking and whether that behavior is congruent with you, your expectations, and the company's reputation and culture. In stage one, person-culture fit is absolutely paramount! It is the bedrock for all of the future stages of growth

---

[27] http://successfulhiring.com/wp-content/uploads/2014/08/s-7.pdf

we'll build on top of it. It should be extremely 'tight' with each person you hire.

Second, you'll be able to determine the fundamental roles and functions you need to help you scope the talent, skills, and capabilities you're looking for. Can they meet the expectations flexibly, creatively, and do so completely? Can they adapt? It helps you develop future post-hire performance development plans.

This information then helps you determine the key metrics. They should be simple, clear, and meaningful so that they are useful and usable.

Borrowing from Gino Wickman in his book _Traction_, does the candidate want the role; do they get the role; can they do the role; and how will their performance be rated? For us, the rating system is simple. Outcomes are considered with the way they were achieved and are given assessment marks for each contribution.

Again, using Vets2PM's performance system to illustrate, the fundamental positions we established beyond myself are daily administration of the business, daily operations of the business, training delivery, career services delivery, and a sales force for covering business-to-consumer (B2C), business-to-business (B2B), and business-to-government (B2G). With these key roles filled, we continuously define and refine these roles. We talk about essential and emerging skills and capabilities, expectations, and needs. We also continuously discuss desired outcomes to maintain flexibility and performance for both individuals and company. This enhances the person-company fit.

Regarding performance, we use a simple "+", "-", or a "+/-" on their performance score card for each period of performance. They rate their performance in major tasks and projects, and so do I. We then talk about the gaps if any, and future expectations. It is driven by the employee, and the results drive their professional development. This keeps behavior consistent, congruent with the company values, mission, and brand, and makes it empowering and autonomous. In fact, my training guru, an Army Captain, often says "I love the freedom of maneuver you provide us Doc!" That's empowered!

We then juxtapose individual behavior and contributions against company performance. Yep, we share our financial statements. We share our values often. We share our decision-making process and tools in the open among the team on weekly virtual synchronization meetings. Our owner-minded employees see what information is really important on the 'score board.' To borrow a great illustration from Jack Stack's book _The Great Game of Business_: Does it take trust? Yes! Does it build it and enhance it? Yes! Does it increase individual and team performance? For us, yes it does. Emphatically!

At Vets2PM, we use the financial statement and balance sheet. On the income statement, we watch the top-line revenue, aggregate expenses, and net income. The balance sheet shows us the cash balance and retained earnings. These 'scores' allow us to assess our shared fundamental activity:

1) "do we sell stuff well (revenue)?"
2) "how expensive is it to sell our stuff well (expenses)?"
3) "do we make any money selling stuff (income)?"
4) "do we use that money (cash) well to insulate us from uncertainty (more about this in a minute)?"; and
5) "do we leave anything to grow our company into the future (retained earnings)?"

Providing these common goals, and the shared, sensitive performance information, both organizational and personal, as well as employee-generated qualitative and quantitative goals for their respective areas of the company, are the three essential characteristics of our high-performing team. Add to these three characteristics pride and ownership, trust, participation, and conflict resolution, and you have the primary characteristics of high-performing teams.[28] The characteristics of high-performing teams means that you have more bandwidth because your team is more mature, durable, resilient, autonomous, capable, responsible, accountable, and able to make decisions congruent with your expectations and the company's culture.

A Bit of Real-Time Business Acumen

Okay, quick side street here regarding my earlier mention of cash on the balance sheet and uncertainty. I have always been a bit of a contrarian…i.e.

---

[28] http://bit.ly/ContinuousLearningHighPerformanceTeams

the guy who usually does the opposite of what the crowd is doing. A specific example that's extremely poignant right now is COVID-19. It is August 2020 as I write this and we are right in the middle of an unprecedented national economic and civil lockdown. Our onsite training revenue vaporized overnight! We brought together the empowered team, each member owns their piece of the business so to speak. Each member of the team makes decisions and evaluates performance information. And each team member asks, "what are we going to do?"

First, we always keep a minimum of six months' salary obligations on hand in case we ever hit a period of no sales, which proved invaluable! When all the gas stations closed so to speak, we had reserve fuel to run on! However, pre-COVID-19, most professionals such as bankers, vendors, accountants, and financial advisors, including some on my own team, say "that's too conservative," or "you should spend some money," or "you should take on more debt to grow!" Planning for the future and keeping emergency cash on hand, I was able to weather COVID and protect my employees and their families. Thank God!

Second, we also keep our debt obligations extremely low and retained earnings high, allowing us to fund growth opportunities quickly, adequately, and sustainably. On our own! Yep, we are still firing on all cylinders. With powerful conviction and creativity! During COVID-19!

Thanks to our strong team and culture, we are able to cover the tribe with food, wood, and shelter, which allows us creative space to: 1) create a new on-demand training platform for the civilian project management market using the same practical, effective training and learning tools we provide our veteran clients, 2) add another training pipeline which we use to service constantly-fluctuating government and government contractor staffs, 3) add another training pipeline which we use to service Department of Defense (DOD) cyber requirements, often referred to as "8570," 4) stand up a B2G division leveraging past commercial and defense contractor performance to diversify our income streams, 5) learn how to repeatably form revenue-generating relationships with other training shops offering complimentary training and hire-out work to retired military personnel and military spouses, and (6) add another professional credential to help even more transitioning military members and veterans by translating their military leadership experience into valuable, universally understood general management language. We will have covered about 40% of all transitioning service members once everything is built and tested; helping even more military veterans achieve meaningful, lucrative post-service intra or entrepreneur careers.

All right, we're merging back on the chapter's highway now.

Initial Growth with Your Nine

You have a clear, well-defined culture. It will be an extension of you. You also know what roles you're looking to fill based on what you need to delegate and what your expectations of performance are around those roles. You understand that capability and fit is more important than specific skills right now, and you have used your behavioral hiring questions to assemble a high-performing team of ownership-minded people. To this responsible, accountable, capable team you can now delegate and coach consistently, which empowers and energizes them through trust, transparency, and autonomy.

Now, you can pivot to growing the company's sales volume and revenue. However, you still need to keep an eye on the two big indicators of how well the company is performing congruent with you, your values, and your expectations: quality and customer service levels. Like all of the other items, yes, you and your team have outlined these. They will be rated "+", "-", and "+/-" as well. You have worked hard to establish your brand, culture, and reputation, and these two key indicators help you assess how well you are being true to this.

We don't want to get lost in metrics, so just identify a couple meaningful ones with your staff. For example, at Vets2PM, we use: 1) customer response time; ours is less than 24 business hours, 2) customer experience ("how satisfied were you with your course? With your instructor?"), and 3) our end-of-course surveys that ask "would you recommend Vets2PM to a fellow service member or veteran?" and "what other services and/or courses could we offer you to meet your professional development needs?" Answers to these questions allow us to assess how we're doing, and how to meet our veteran clients' needs. Continuously.

Once your culture is created, you will need to communicate your culture clearly and often. You will do this through systemic, consistent coaching, empowerment, and behavior modeling. I do it in emails. I discuss it using examples from the previous month on our weekly virtual calls. We use it in performance discussions. I talk about how I use our culture to drive my behavior and decision-making using actual examples from my workdays. The idea is alignment, alignment, and alignment. Employee behavior and decision-making must align with, and remain tight to, your company's culture as the team and business grows. This facilitates delegation.

Conclusion

Our example demonstrated the essential things necessary that you, the solopreneur, need to know to grow your team beyond you...beyond your kitchen table and through stage one of your company's growth, which is 1-10 employees.

They are:

1) Create a strong, clear culture of mission, vision, values, decision-making, and integrity.
2) Define clear roles, functions, and goals complete with the general skills and capabilities that flow from them.
3) Identify concise, essential, meaningful performance expectations.
4) Design and implement systems to consistently flow feedback to and from team members and facilitate decision-making congruent with the company to steward scarce resources, brand, and reputation.

These nine other employees are key to your success in growing the company because you have to be able to delegate to grow. Yes, you do know it all, but no, you can't do it all if you want to grow. Start practicing now! Set up the processes, systems, and a team that can help you!

Happy building!

* * *

Eric "Doc" Wright, PhD, is a decorated military veteran, serial founder of Vets2PM, LLC and VPMMA 501(c)3, business philosopher and linguist, and 3x Amazon best selling author. He authored the book _How To Speak Civilian Fluently: And Prove It!_ to teach veterans and the civilian labor force the language of _management_ and prove it with their internationally-recognized Certified Manager credential from the nonprofit Institute of Certified Professional Managers. His work in _management_ fluency has helped tens of thousands of military veterans, managers, contractors, and government personnel achieve meaningful, lucrative careers and businesses! Vets2PM is the 2019 and 2020 Department of Labor HIRE Vets Gold Award Winner in the small business category for its veteran hiring initiatives!

Secure your small business coaching with Doc at:
https://federal-access.com/ericdocwright/; and

Find him on LinkedIn as *docwright2012* at
www.vets2pm.com/blog.

Next Steps

Get some coaching - whether it's one of the authors in this book or someone else – strengthen your business maturity and request help! If you don't know where to start, you can sign up for a *free Business Breakthrough session* on our website. It takes about 5 minutes to fill out the form. Just visit: https://rsmfederal.com/breakthroughcoaching

Finally, thank you for picking up this book. We really appreciate it! I cannot thank you enough for helping get our message out to the masses. In that spirit, if you enjoyed this book and know someone who could benefit from it, please make them aware of it or just buy them a copy.

Thank you again! Don't hesitate to contact us if you have questions.

One Last Thing... or Two?

There are 6 of us that spent a year writing this book! We want to thank you for trusting us with your time.

If you enjoyed and gained value from this book, we would be *very grateful* if you help us in return.

1. **Post a review on Amazon.** Even if you did not buy this book on Amazon, you can still leave a review! This is the most important and valuable thing you can do for our team of authors!

2. **Take a picture of yourself holding this book and post the picture to LinkedIn** *and* say why you enjoyed the book. Publishing and marketing a book is difficult. Our ability to share your picture with our network is 100 times more powerful than our own marketing. (Just make sure to tag us – Russ Barnes, Jenny Clark, Emily Harman, Joshua Frank, Michael LeJeune, Eric "Doc" Wright.)

Your support really does make a difference. We read and respond to all LinkedIn posts personally.

Thanks again for your support!

Other Resources

Game Changers for Government Contractors

#1 Amazon Bestseller
Visit https://bit.ly/GovConGameChangers

An Insider's Guide to Winning Government Contracts

#1 Amazon Bestseller
Visit https://bit.ly/GovConInsidersGuide

Federal Access (FA) Platform

The flagship solution of RSM Federal. Federal Access (FA) is an award winning and nationally-recognized acceleration platform that has helped companies win more than $2.8 Billion in government contracts.

FA has more than 300 essential documents, 100+ training videos, and industry leading Subject Matter Expertise (SME) for government contractors. You can start your journey with us today for $29 by visiting https://federal-access.com/govconexpertsbook

Podcast
Game Changers for Government Contractors

Available on any podcasting app. Just search for Game Changers for Government Contractors. This podcast is the #1 podcast in the Nation for small business government contractors.

Every month, industry subject matter experts provide game-changing strategies for winning government contracts. Game Changers was designed BY government contractors FOR government contractors. Visit https://bit.ly/GovConPodcast

Podcast
Onward Podcast

Emily Harman shares authentic conversations about how to move forward when confronted with challenges. The podcast covers a broad range of topics including living an authentic life, recovering from drug abuse, overcoming a spinal cord injury, losing a child, surviving depression, living with anxiety and more. Just search for Onward Podcast on any app. Visit https://emilyharman.com/onwardpodcast/

Podcast
Navigating GovCon

Jenny Clark talks all things pricing, costs, and being competitive in the world of GovCon. Ror more information and to listen to episodes, visit https://solvability.com/category/govcon-podcast/.

Podcast
Purposefully Profitable Podcast

The Trial-and-Error Turnpike is the Road to Ruin. Learn the Purposefully Profitability Principles provided by the Profitability Professor Dr. Russ Barnes on the Purposefully Profitable Podcast and start making progress on the Path to Prosperity. Find this podcast on apple podcasts by visiting https://podcasts.apple.com/us/podcast/purposefully-profitable-podcast/id1275323682

Your Amazing Itty Bitty® Small Business for Service Members Book: 15 Things You Need to Know to Be Purposefully Profitable

Visit https://www.amazon.com/dp/B0755N3CF9

Doc's Transition Classroom

Each episode of Doc's Translation Classroom presents just one of the 300+ terms contained in the book on _How To Speak Civilian Fluently: And Prove It!_ So be sure to Subscribe to our Vets2PM YouTube channel to catch every episode.

Connect with us on LinkedIn

If you gained value from the content and concepts in this book, we highly suggest that you connect to EVERY one of the authors on LinkedIn. We all provide similar value via articles and posts on a regular basis. Be sure and mention that you heard about us via this book!

About RSM Federal

The Art and Science of Government Sales™

RSM Federal is an award-winning coaching and consulting firm that works with small, mid-tier, and large companies to accelerate their understanding of the government market and learn how to position for and successfully win government contracts - with exceptional results. Our clients have won over $2.8 Billion in government contracts and more than $30 Billion in MATOCs since 2008.

Providing the **Art and Science of Government Sales**™, RSM Federal has quickly become a nationally trusted educator, trainer, coach, and consultant to other companies, associations, and coalitions.

We emphasize basic and advanced strategies tailored specifically for your company to accelerate success and revenue. We leverage a proven combination of industry expertise and measurable strategies to deliver cost-effective and high-value results for our clients.

With nationally recognized and award-winning expertise and hundreds of resources, tactics, templates, and step-by-step strategies, your company can immediately accelerate your marketing, prospecting, sales, teaming, and proposal activities - literally overnight.

About Michael LeJeune

Editor-in-Chief

MICHAEL LEJEUNE is a Partner with RSM Federal and the Program Manager for the Federal Access Platform. He is an award-winning business coach and author. He has been consulting and mentoring companies in the government market for nearly twenty years.

Michael specializes in breakthrough and executive coaching. He works primarily with companies that are either new to the market or have plateaued and don't know what to do next.

You have likely heard Michael on the nation's leading government contractor podcast - Game Changers for Government Contractors. Michael started this podcast with co-host Joshua Frank in 2016. Thousands of contractors listen to Game Changers every month. Game Changers is available on every podcasting app.

Michael served four years in the Army at Ft. Hood. First in the 2nd Armor Division and then with the 4th Infantry division from 1995 to 1999. Michael received numerous awards while working on the FORCE XXI project for the Army testing new equipment and technologies. This is how Michael was introduced to government contracting.

Michael started his corporate career in 1999 with GTE/General Dynamics in the highly competitive collaboration space. His primary clients were DoD, Intelligence Agencies, and the Joint Forces Commands.

Michael currently resides in the small town (5,500 people) of Monticello, IL with his wife, two daughters, and two puppies. He hates the cold and looks forward to moving to someplace warm after his youngest daughter finishes high school.

About Joshua P. Frank

Executive Editor

JOSHUA P. FRANK is the Founder and Managing partner for RSM Federal. Bestselling author, trainer, and award-winning GovCon business coach with 30+ years in the government market, Josh is referred to as the Professor of Government Sales. A recognized authority on government sales, he speaks nationally on business strategy and business acceleration. His training sessions, highly educational and thought-provoking, are consistently rated the top sessions at national conferences and events. His training, with thousands of testimonials, is consistently rated as being real-world, highly educational, and thought provoking.

Mr. Frank is author of Amazon's #1 bestseller _An Insider's Guide to Winning Government Contracts – Real World Strategies, Lessons, and Recommendations_, the highest selling GovCon book on Amazon today.

He was awarded Veteran Business Owner of the Year by the Small Business Administration (_a first for a business coach_) and the National Industry Small Business Advocate of the Year award by the Society of American Military Engineers (SAME).

A former military intelligence officer, Masters in Management Information Systems (MIS) and a Master's in Business Administration (MBA). Connect with Mr. Frank on LinkedIn
https://www.linkedin.com/in/joshuapfrank

He lives in St. Louis, Missouri with his wife, son, and daughter.

Author Websites

michaellejeune.com and authorjoshfrank.com

Learn more about RSM Federal

rsmfederal.com

Learn more about Federal Access

https://federal-access.com/govconexpertsbook

FREE podcasts for government contractors at

https://bit.ly/GovConPodcast

Made in United States
Orlando, FL
09 February 2022

14587627R00126